IN-ARMS CARRYING

A practical guide for comfortable baby carrying

Mel Cyrille

Table of Contents

Introduction

Let me start by saying that this is a subject which I imagine I'll be studying for the rest of my life. I've barely scratched the surface, and what I've found is incredible! The more I carry my children and the more research I do, the more I learn about carrying.

It's frustrating not having topic-specific research, articles and general information to guide you when you're looking to learn more about the how's and why's. It's also frustrating not being able to back up your own knowledge with "scientifically proven facts", which tend to be held in much higher regard than lived experience.

I've not let this stop me though - the contents of this book are backed up by research specific to individual elements related to carrying, and comparisons seen in studies with similarities to in-arms carrying. I've been very careful which data I've used, as, although there are many more studies and papers I could have included; I wanted to stay away from certain things.

For example, I don't think it's useful to compare data across species for the most part. Some may be useful for saying "oh look, that's similar", but beyond that, it's just trying to use something not relevant to humans to try and back up a point. Also, for the most part, I don't use studies that have been conducted with very different cultures to the UK. This is because people around the world lead very different lives; therefore our "normal" can be the polar opposite to others.

Even if we had proper normal data for people in the UK (as in, physiologically normal), I'm sure we would find many differences in bodies across cultures as we've adapted to the terrain, weather and daily demands of where we live, so likely have cultural quirks.

It isn't all fruitless though – we can look at things like the physical development of babies and young children, pinpoint where and when things start to go wrong, what certain professionals advise with regards to our health (e.g. osteopaths and chiropractors), general observation of people and dyads around us etc. I like to "back up" what I can with scientific data, as it caters to the scientifically-minded people and it also feels good to see your beliefs being "proven". However, I know that scientific studies can be problematic, and also are limited in what they can give us.

Looking at nature is my preference - seeing people in their normal environments, observing normal behaviours, watching the unique interactions between baby/child and caregiver – these are the things which give a three-dimensional story.

Hopefully though, there will one day be carrying-specific research, which will provide proof of what we already know, and hopefully uncover a whole lot more! There is definitely a place for research, especially when it comes to changing our approach to carrying and the opinion of society in general.

In this book we'll explore just how intricate the carrying process is, especially when it comes to clinging behaviour. I'll hold a magnifying glass up to the many ways in which lots of us have bodies less suited to biologically normal carrying, and discuss ways of correcting this. We'll look at the differences between "active" and "passive" carrying, and how they impact on our bodies and clinging behaviour.

As there's very little out there written on in-arms carrying, this is a work stepping into largely unfamiliar territory. It has taken a great deal of courage and determination to write this book, with my not having things like a degree in biology or biomechanics, or another scientific/medical background, but my belief in the importance of carrying and the explosion of information I've collated on the subject meant it had to be done.

This book is a summary of my thoughts, experiences and research into in-arms carrying. I hope it sparks an interest for you in your parenting, line of work or personal interest. Thank you for buying this book and I hope you enjoy reading it!

Mel

Disclaimer

The information presented in this book is accurate as far as the author is aware, and is evidence-based. It is not a substitute for any medical advice you have received, and using methods described in this book should be done so at yours and your healthcare provider's discretion. The author accepts no liability for any damage or adverse events. You are responsible for your baby/child and should make informed decisions as to how you carry. If in doubt, it's advisable to seek advice from a relevant healthcare professional.

I do not hold any medical qualifications. The content of this book is based on what I've learned on my adult learning journey so far, which includes biology and many topics related to baby development, along with my lived experiences with my children, plus observations of the caregivers and babies/children I've worked with over the past 5+ years.

If you have any concerns about your baby/child's development or if they have a pre-existing condition, please seek advice from a medical professional.

Chapter 1

My Story

I'd like to share with you my journey of discovery of the wonderful world of in-arms carrying.

In 2004 I gave birth to my first baby, Niamh, and I used a pram almost exclusively for transporting out of the house until she could walk (plus a brief encounter with a Tomy carrier). As I hadn't learned to drive, I walked most places and used public transport for longer journeys. With no plans to learn to drive in the foreseeable future, I had her walking short distances from 2 months after she learned to walk, and gradually increased this until she walked everywhere with me. I didn't carry her much in-arms.

Carrying wasn't something I associated with development, or really enjoyed much beyond the early days and the snuggles as she got older. As she got heavier it became more of an inconvenience than anything else, as she was heavy and the act of carrying felt cumbersome.

In 2010 I birthed my second baby, Logan. When I was pregnant with him I was introduced to a whole new world of slings, courtesy of one of my cousins, Cerys. 2 days before she gave birth to her first baby I found out I was pregnant. Cerys used slings with her daughter and I could see how different they were and how comfortable they both looked. Based on how happy they both looked and the products she was using, I ended up buying a stretchy and a woven wrap when I was pregnant.

Logan's first trip out after he was born was in the stretchy wrap, to a play Niamh was in, and I was nervous about how it would go. Needless to say, he absolutely loved it and I was amazed at how content he was in it. He spent most of the time asleep, and when he woke up on the walk home – after an initial panic – I managed to feed him on the go! This was my true realisation about how babies are designed to be carried.

When we tried using the pram he would cry and it further confirmed this understanding that babies want and need to be carried. We used the pram all of 3 times before putting it up in the loft and were both converted.

Tom's first babywearing experience

Logan was in the sling whenever we went out, and was worn a fair bit inside the house. Naps happened at a click of the fingers when he was in there, and I was able to get things done. I carried him in the sling everywhere out and about, and regularly at home. I didn't do much in the way of carrying in-arms with him – slings replaced my arms most of the time for general carrying. I defaulted to the sling as it was so much easier.

As he got older, I was concerned about him not having the regular walking outdoors that his sister had, and worried that he wouldn't get used to the distance walking like she had. But it was much easier to have him in the wrap. He loved being up there, and was sooooo slooooow when he walked (you know, all those interesting things to look at and learn about!). Ultimately, I was impatient and it was convenience over the benefits of walking, with appointments to attend and places to be.

Funnily enough, I had nothing to worry about with him. He gradually transitioned to walking, and easily walked long distances. He's always been a very active baby and child so I think he got his exercise in other ways which enabled him to take on distance walking with ease. This is a great example of how something can be lacking in one area but is made up (to a certain extent) in another. No, you can't replace the exact movements and ranges of motion with different movements, but some things can help bridge the gap.

I noticed with him that he felt so much heavier in-arms than I remembered Niamh ever being, yet he was lighter than she was. At the time I thought I was noticing how heavy he was because slings made him feel so light in comparison. I didn't make the connection that it was because my arms weren't getting a regular carrying "workout" with him, so they weren't adapting to his weight. The lack of regular in-arms carrying also meant that I used my body more to take some of the weight. Carrying wasn't very appealing when I had babywearing, and I really didn't think much of it.

So Logan was carried in-arms even less than Niamh, as I had a replacement for my arms – slings! Thankfully though, this wasn't the end and as time went on and I learned more which I was able to adapt for him as an older child and his clinging abilities developed incredibly well despite a lack of carrying as a baby.

My light bulb moment and progression on my journey with in-arms carrying really begins with my 3rd baby, Xander. He taught me incredible amounts about in-arms carrying, was the catalyst for me teaching Logan to be an active participant long after the natural progression of carrying begins and set me down the path to writing this book.

Xander was a learning experience from the get-go. I used wraps with him but he soon let me know that he was most comfortable in a ring sling, which is one of my least favourites personally! I got an inkling then that he was going to challenge my comfort zones and teach me lots – and so he has and still does.

I also practiced natural infant hygiene (or elimination communication) with him from birth which gave me a different perspective to understanding babies. I'd started at 5 months with Logan, and he taught me a lot too, but this time it was different. I now had an insight into how babies communicate from birth, and Xander had something he wanted to teach me beyond how to trust a newborn baby to know what their body needs.

This letting go of control and placing full trust in a tiny, seemingly helpless, human being is a struggle against societal conditioning. In letting go and listening to him, I began to notice other subtle ways he communicated, including how to hold him that I hadn't noticed with my other babies this early on.

I found it easier to carry in a more instinctive way, rather than feeling like I was hauling a sack of baby around. As I carried him more and more in-arms I noticed his better clinging capabilities in comparison to Logan. I was usually only using a sling out of the house, and even then I noticed myself not bothering for things like trips to the corner shop. I used to joke I got lazier; I couldn't be bothered to put the sling on! In fact, it was the opposite, even if it didn't feel like it at the time. The more you carry in-arms, the easier it becomes. Your strength and endurance builds up and you get to a point where carrying actually becomes more convenient at times than a carrying aid.

I first trained as a Babywearing Consultant when I was newly pregnant with Xander. In the Western babywearing educational field, there are some interesting beliefs to do with positioning and babies' hips and spines. Some of these beliefs and teachings have evolved over the years but others have held firm. With the spine, it's widely taught that babies and young children should be positioned with a curved spine in the sling until at least 9 months old,[1] if not older. It's true that it's ideal for babies' spines to go back to a "C" shape at rest, but when they are awake and active they tend to sit with a straighter spine, even when very young.

I'd also been taught that it was important to avoid any pressure on the spine, as this was harmful to their development, but active carrying tends to require your arm to support their back rather than let them sit on your forearm. When I transitioned to this way of holding (them sitting on my forearm), I found myself arching my back/rib-thrusting. It didn't feel right, but the thought that I was protecting my baby's spine by doing this overruled my concern for my own body. It's funny, isn't it? That drive to do what's best for your baby or child – hard-wired into you – that can sometimes override common sense!

So, here I was, now carrying my baby in a way that was having a negative impact on my body. What did I do? Well, first of all, I played around with how I was holding my body. I soon realised that I *needed* to create this bracing point as without an arm on his back, his support had vanished. He hadn't had this period of transition from a hand on the back to short periods of time without it to begin to gain control for himself. He'd come to expect support in a certain area, so would lean in to me in the way he was used to.

I did lots of research on spinal development and studied carrying behaviours of people around the world. I also looked at all the different ways babies experience spinal pressure, from birth onwards. I furthered my learning by reading articles, research and books about other primates and their clinging behaviours. I knew better than to compare directly to humans, but I used this knowledge to explore the similarities and possibilities with humans.

I ended up getting very frustrated with the lack of writing, research, visual aids and recorded history of human carrying. I began writing down my observations, recording my thoughts and experiences, and put feelers out in 2015 with my blog post "In-arms Carrying",[2] which was an introduction to the concept for parents and babywearing educators. It included a video (and another, after Isaac was born) for what I believe is the closest imitation to an in-arms chest-to-chest front carry with a sling.

As I became more aware of the importance of posture and alignment in carrying, I began reading more of Katy Bowman's work.[3] Already a barefoot shoe convert, I began working on my body, with special attention to how I was holding myself when carrying in-arms and in slings. I learned about how loads impact our posture and alignment and suddenly things seemed a lot clearer. Katy had also spoken briefly about carrying children in-arms, and was my first introduction to an "educated" point of view on carrying (Katy is a biomechanist).

What I found though, was information about what I call passive in-arms carrying. Katy is a big fan of freedom of movement for children, and recognises the need to encourage normal movement patterns for them. The insights that she shares publicly about carrying them, however, are focused on the person carrying, and how to protect their body. I learned about how to protect my shoulders,[4] that it was important to resist creating a "shelf" for them to sit on with your ribs or hips,[5] and that it was beneficial to build up strength in your biceps as this was where your carrying strength and endurance came from.

She helped me to carry Xander much more comfortably and encouraged me to work on my body as a whole to get better posture and range of motion within my joints. This was all a stepping stone to what I've learned since about baby carrying. I highly recommend reading Katy's books. She's written several of them about different things, and you can learn lots about ways to improve your posture and alignment, up your movement quota, improve your living spaces, heal diastasis recti, learn about the pelvic floor and much more.

Xander was a baby who wanted to be held in-arms a lot and by the time he reached 2 years old he rarely wanted to go in the sling. He didn't want to walk though - he wanted to be carried in-arms, all the time. I felt like I'd brought this upon myself by using the sling less and less – which I had, but it really wasn't the negative thing it felt like. Amazingly, this coincided with me taking my driving test and passing, so the effects of this were considerably less than they would have been if I'd still had to walk and use public transport to get to places. I also robbed myself of the opportunity to learn more as I would have had to adapt to his carrying needs without the convenience of a car.

Unfortunately this also had a negative impact on my body. Learning to drive was certainly liberating, but it was a huge contribution to a more sedentary lifestyle. I used it as a way to cut down on carrying and walking, enjoying this wonderful convenience. It also wreaked havoc on my posture as I found myself sitting on my tailbone rather than my sitting bones and slouching forwards whenever I drove.

So my learning to drive meant my in-arms carrying was less than it would have been, but still happened around the house and every time I left the house or car with him, as he would melt into the pavement if someone refused to carry him. It was incredibly frustrating at the time, and I wondered if in-arms carrying was worse for him in terms of encouraging independent walking than pram or sling use may be. But as time went on his need for being carried became clearer. Speech delay and frustrations meant he needed the closeness and feeling of security more than ever. For him, being held in-arms met that need better than a sling could.

During Xander's first couple of years he taught me how to hold my body to make carrying more comfortable and helped me to de-school some of what I'd been taught about baby carrying. Although he taught me how to carry in mainly passive positions, he (along with my copious reading) taught me how to do it well, and he laid the foundation for my work going forwards with in-arms carrying.

When I was pregnant with Isaac, my fourth baby, I found myself paying closer attention to the changes in my body. I was now aware of the potential injuries I could sustain through posture and positional carrying. I needed to work harder to adjust to the changes in both my body and posture as my weight and shape evolved. It was an ongoing learning experience as I navigated the possibilities with this ever-changing body.

My exercise of choice before and during pregnancy was trampolining, which – as a form of gymnastics - requires good posture and alignment. This helped (and is still helping) with my ongoing work to reverse the damage I'd done over the last couple of decades. It also helped me with being a little less sedentary, which was much needed.

When I was 4 months pregnant we went on holiday. As my shape had changed I was finding I was carrying Xander much more on my hip. When I was pregnant with him, Logan was over a year younger than Xander was now, plus he was very light for his age. I was able to carry and babywear Logan on my front until around 24 weeks pregnant, but Xander was over a year older, plus he was of an average weight for his age. On holiday, I knew I would be carrying him more than usual, and that he preferred me recently, so I wouldn't have much chance to share the load. As he was still sling-averse, I predicted I would come back home needing an osteopath appointment for a hip out of alignment. I was right.

Xander required a lot of carrying that week, and (3 years later) I still vividly remember the moment the full damage was done. We were walking down Newquay high street, me with Xan on my right hip, enjoying the sunshine, when I began to feel this stretching. You know when you stretch a muscle just beyond its comfort zone? That cosy place of "Oooo! I didn't know I could stretch that little bit further!"? Well, I was there, but a split second later something strange happened. I started feeling what I can only describe as a crackling/pulling/separating feeling. It didn't hurt until that sensation stopped. Before long I felt the pain deep in my muscles around my lower spine.

Sure enough, the next day I had pain in both my lower spine and right hip. Once I got home I arranged an appointment with my osteopath. He guessed what had happened as soon as he'd seen and felt my misalignment.

This incident made me much more careful about how I was carrying, but also instilled a caution in me about hip carrying. I felt like I had additional ammo now about the perils of carrying on your hip - especially in a baby carrier, where the weight is distributed in an abnormal fashion when compared to in-arms. I still carried Xander on my hip occasionally, but veered towards carrying him on my back, pleading with him to walk, and transitioning him to Tom being the person he wanted to carry him.

After pregnancy I started using hip carries again with the older boys. The injury during pregnancy taught me how to carry more safely on my hip and what things to look out for as warning signs. I looked for information about the potential damage we can cause our spines by carrying loads on our hips and in other places on our body if we're not maintaining awareness of, and correcting, posture and alignment. I found that research backed up my theories.[6] [7] [8]

Isaac has very much been an in-arms baby. It wasn't intentional on my part, but it was on his. Being in a much more comfortable place communicating with a newborn after Xander's EC teachings, I was much more aware of other, newer (to me) forms of communication.

I was paying more attention to how he sat on my body, his natural positions, how he behaved, what his micro- and macro-adjustments were, and my interest was piqued seeing as I'd been led to believe that babies were underdeveloped, frail, and needing their caregivers to provide careful support and be their arms and legs. What Isaac taught me was that babies are as advanced physically as they are communicatively, right from the get go.

I remembered Dr. Kirkilionis' insights into infant carrying and reflexes, and the rest, as they say, is history. From here I began to understand how some primitive reflexes related to in-arms carrying, and that we've been looking at carrying from the wrong angle. We tend to compare babies to apes, noticing similarities in behaviours, and that's great but when we focus on human babies in all their amazing glory we start to see things that we hadn't seen before.

I also started to see the spread-squat position and variations of it everywhere, from holding Isaac in-arms to relieve himself, to children moving and playing. Intrigued, I set out to find out why this leg position is prevalent at each stage of development.

During this time, I learned so much from Isaac about active carrying. The understanding of infant reflexes told me that the logical next step in development would be conscious clinging. Not the wrapping round of legs, but actual clinging. However, I wasn't seeing this behaviour around me. Everywhere I looked, it was passive carrying. I also began to notice the straight-legged behaviour of so many babies and children when carried in-arms. Had we lost the ability to cling? Surely not, as older children can cling on in piggy-backs, and even adults can wrap themselves around something and hold on!

And so the research went deeper. Why do we carry passively much of the time? *Are* babies able to cling (properly), or are the clinging reflexes, in fact, useless? A pattern of sedentary behaviour kept coming up, and things were getting clearer. We carry passively as a default because our bodies are used to being passive. We're also taught that babies are helpless, and that we need to handle them with great care.

Now, Isaac was getting bigger and stronger, and his conscious clinging was getting better and better. It seemed that if you work with the natural instincts, they develop seamlessly into conscious, voluntary holding on. I was seeing great similarities with elimination communication, in that if you work with their involuntary communication of needing to go from a very young age, the awareness and ability to communicate continues and develops into conscious and voluntary communication.

With this in mind, I started to think about how the majority of babies in the UK are in nappies and aren't helped to eliminate away from their body until potty training commences, any time from around 12 months to 4 years (averaging between age 2 and 3). If the awareness of needing the toilet can be suppressed then re-emerge spontaneously or be taught at a later date, how about clinging behaviour?

And so I began consciously working with my older boys to put this theory to the test. Both had the advantage of being used to the ergonomical in-arms position of the spread-squat through babywearing and (mainly passive) in-arms carrying, so that was a bonus! The thing now was to make a shift from passive to active carrying.

At this point in time I had a small baby obviously, so he was held the most. It tended to be when we went out as a family that they got to practice. Over a short period of time they got used to working with me - it was an organic process of them gradually holding on for longer periods of time, and going back to passive holds as they would tire.

At almost 5 and 6.5 years old at the time of publishing, they *need* to be active participants if they want a ride - I need to protect my body, and they get the added bonus of being carried for longer! They don't always adopt an active position straight away (especially Xander), but will soon change when prompted. In comparison, Isaac (20 months old) automatically goes into an active position unless he's tired.

Although Logan and Xander have both benefited from being taught to cling at a later age, Logan, as an active child, easily surpassed Xander in clinging ability. Xander is not into physical activity. To me this shows how it's not always nurture that has the biggest impact – nature (our inborn skills and tendencies) can define part of our response.

During Isaac's reflexive carrying phase he'd been gaining upper body strength so was held in more passive positions, with arm off the spine. These positions supported his lower body as his upper body was strengthening, but allowed the freedom of movement for his upper body.

This meant that when he was very little he could straighten his neck as and when he wanted (with a hand supporting his upper back when needed), but also snuggle in when he wanted or needed to rest. With the completion of constant head and neck control, he could now start strengthening his upper back, with full support for his lower limbs and some support of the lower spine with a hand.

As he gained trunk control and was sitting straighter, the support went to the upper back for active carrying focused more on the lower back and limbs with some support for his legs at times. As he developed further, and could sit unaided, the support moved to his lower back. Interestingly, this all correlates with babies' spinal development stages, and he thrived. He made this beautiful transition from reflexive carrying to conscious carrying.

As the months went on, and he progressed to crawling, cruising and walking, his clinging capacity grew stronger. He could be held in active positions for longer periods of time, and this was proving to me the cleverness of how they need to be carried less as they learn to move independently (crawling, walking etc.), and how they cling on better the older and heavier they get, enabling carrying to continue at the times when they need it. It's a perfect progression from the in-arms phase to independence of transportation.

One of the keys with responsive carrying is to be aware of the baby's energy levels and respond as instinctively as possible to how they want and need to be carried. In-arms it's easy to shift positions regularly, and to switch between active and passive carrying.

For me personally, this journey into the world of in-arms carrying has been fantastic. Not only has it helped me to understand better how babies and children develop, but it's encouraged me to spend time trying to reverse the damage I've done to my own body over the years.

Also, as I worked harder to keep correcting my posture when carrying the older boys passively, I got stronger. It's much harder work (in a good way!) on your arm muscles, and your core, when you're not shifting your body out of alignment to create a "shelf"! Active carrying enabled me to focus even more on my posture and alignment as there was less focus on supporting their weight.

I know I will be working on my posture and alignment for the rest of my life, but the knowledge that it will help protect my body and keep me stronger and healthier keeps me going. Don't think that I'm this hardcore posture and alignment person though - I do nowhere near the amount of work I know I should, and make lifestyle choices which are counter-productive, but I'm at peace with that for now.

Chapter 2

The Original Baby Carrier

Human babies were born to be carried. Born with underdeveloped muscular-skeletal systems, they rely on caregivers to transport them as well as to take care of them and keep them alive.

It comes as no surprise that our arms and bodies are the original baby carrier - our arms are made for carrying and our bodies shaped to facilitate the rider as perfectly as an interlocking jigsaw piece, no matter our size, shape or gender. Although that may be the case, it makes sense to presume that some form of baby carrying aid would have been invented fairly quickly, to enable parents and carers to do be more efficient with daily tasks and demands, and to make journeying distances easier.

Although modern-day technological advances make carrying less needed, and - arguably - less appealing, we do still thankfully carry in-arms and carriers. Unfortunately, in the process of perceived advances in society, we're losing the skill of aligned and active physiological carrying. Carrying tends to be seen as something we do *to* or *for* a baby/child, rather than a reciprocal activity.

Carrying in England in this day and age tends to veer towards passive, and many people find that they get aches and pains if they carry for too long. Some people even end up harming their body in certain ways; for example, altering their alignment through sticking their hip out or moving their hips and/or ribs forwards.

Other ways we may not be doing ourselves any favours is by not utilising babies' inborn clinging ability, and helping them develop this skill as they grow. If a baby isn't doing its fair share of the work, then the person doing the carrying is picking up the extra weight and effort. This means we have to work harder to carry, and can contribute to the unwanted side affects of aches and misalignment.

A lot of us are also in a perpetual cycle of using baby containers (e.g. prams, slings, baby bouncers), so don't get used to the weight of the baby in our arms, which means when we need to pick them up they feel like a heavy lump, so we use these devices more often which makes us less equipped to hold them comfortably, so we use our bodies to brace them on, and round and round it goes. So how did we end up in this cycle, and what can we do to reverse it? Let's begin by looking at baby carrying through the ages in the UK and Europe.

A brief history

This should really be called "A lack of history", as in English history it's hard to get a clear picture of actual day-to-day baby carrying in the past. There seems to be very little written information to do with holding babies, and what I've found is to do with the cradle position, the "classic" baby-holding position.

The internet is a fantastic place for finding information, photographs, drawings and paintings. It's a frustrating place when there isn't much out there specific to what you're looking for though! Why is there a lack of information and imagery to do with baby carrying? Well, for a start, let's think about what subjects might have been of interest to the average historian? Not the day-to-day life of women/families for most! We find the extent of this limited information when we try to research the history of baby care. If you want to know about wars, great! But raising human beings? Not beyond the basics.

Also, drawing and painting are skills. How many artists were there at any given time, and how many of their works have survived over the centuries? Add to this the way our history has been recorded from before the technological era. History was written by men, to talk about things they felt were important (and written to favour them, of course). Then add to this a woman's place in society, meaning her work wasn't held in as high regard as a man's. How many famous female artists versus male artists do you know of throughout history?

Obviously this makes it difficult to paint a history of how we carried our babies and much ends up being speculation. Similar to babywearing history in the UK, we know it happened, we have some paintings, drawings and photographs for reference, but they're a rarity. Another reason for this is because history tends to focus on the upper classes. We know that richer people tended to employ people to look after their babies (and at one point used slaves), even so far as to have them wet nurse.

But all is not lost - we just have to approach the subject from a different angle to get an idea of the history of carrying, even if we are unable to find out clearly *how* babies were carried. We can do this by researching popular parenting advice and practices through different eras. This helps by bringing up questions about what effect they may have had on carrying babies/children, and how carrying was viewed.

What we do know about "commoner" child-rearing is that baby care went through different phases during the ages. During Tudor times, swaddling was very popular. The newborn baby would be wrapped in linen bands from head to toe to ensure they would grow straight and not end up deformed, and they would endure this daily until they were 8 or 9 months old.[1] Of course, they would be unwrapped to change the absorbent materials used to catch urine and faeces, and to be cleaned too. Contrary to popular belief, there wasn't a huge aversion to hygiene when it came to babies, nor were they starved of love and affection.[2] They would be bathed regularly and spend time bonding with their caregiver.

As they grew more active, they would be unbound for longer

periods of time to crawl around, and I think it's safe to say that they would be carried unbound also. Whilst they were bound though, they would not be able to be held in a way where they would sit on the caregiver's body. A big question is, did the very nature of swaddling (compressing the limbs in ways they weren't designed to be) have any affect on carrying?

I wonder how sustained periods of straightening affected the movement of the legs and hips. The natural reflexes wouldn't be stimulated, and there would be no freedom of movement, which is a big part of infant development. We also know that tight swaddling can be a risk factor for developmental dysplasia of the hips.[3] [4] [5] [6] With regular swaddling over this long course of time, it would seem plausible that carrying may have been affected, if just for the lack of being held in the sitting position. Also, within the upper classes where wet nursing was commonplace, it's been suggested that babies were swaddled for longer periods and even neglected,[7] which suggests that babies born to those with money were likely carried less.

The opinion towards swaddling began to fall in 17th century England as there was an association of neglect attached to it. This is attributed to wet nurses leaving babies for extended periods without cleaning or comforting them. Soon, physicians started criticizing the practice and people began to swaddle less and less.

William Cadogan - an 18th century physician and writer about childcare - called for the end of swaddling completely. He urged people to consider the effect the tight bindings had on both the limbs and the bowels, and suggested that the lack of movement would mean weak limbs, which wouldn't be well equipped to withstand the pressure from the weight of the body. This seems to suggest that swaddling was used for extensive periods of time, even if regular breaks were given.

In the 20th century, there was still a view that babies needed to be self-reliant. In a 1911 book "A Handbook of obstetric nursing for nurses, students and mothers"[8], mothers are advised to tend only to the basic needs of their baby, lest they become a "little tyrant" from being spoiled! This meant feeding and cleaning them, but not giving them too much attention, so not holding them and cuddling them too much.

It wasn't until Dr. Benjamin Spock's book "The Common Sense Book of Baby and Child Care" was published that people really started to change their way of thinking about babies. His call for parents to treat babies as individuals and show them more affection saw a shift towards more responsive parenting.

So although we have a general idea about childcare ideas over the ages and how these may have affected carrying, we're still lacking the information about how they *were* carried, and when it happened. To find this out, it seems that we'd need to refer to visual examples. Unfortunately, this is also not so easy to uncover.

When you look at photos and paintings before photography was accessible and affordable to the general public, there's a definite theme that runs through the ages - posing. I have a couple of theories why we don't have much in the way of day-to-day "life with a baby" imagery, and why most show poses.

First of all, like I've already said, the cost of cameras and to develop the film would have made photography inaccessible to many people. If your family were well-off enough to be able to afford this, what would you use your camera for? As family pictures through the ages show, photography at home tended to be for family portraits.

Post-Victorian era, we start to see the odd photograph here and there of a person carrying a baby or child in-arms that isn't in a portrait-style. Babies and children are held mainly in passive holds, and yes, the pram has been around for quite a while, and becoming more accessible, but have we really lost the knowledge of in-arms carrying so quickly? I don't think so. We tend to change our carrying when we're moving and when we're standing still. While moving, there's a tendency to straighten out more and when we're standing still is when more thrusting seems to go on.

When we get closer to the 1990's, pictures of carrying in-arms are more prevalent and as time goes on, reaching the social media and celebrity age, there are lots more to see. There are a couple of clear, strong themes here - passive carrying and/or the person carrying putting their body in various misalignments.

Single-use disposable cameras made photography more accessible. Digital photography has only relatively recently been accessible to the majority, with increasingly affordable digital cameras and camera phones. This, along with the social media and internet age has meant there's an abundance of photos and many ways to share images across the world.

Obviously, in a pre-internet age, this ability to share pictures far and wide wasn't available. Also, how photographs have been lost, either from being thrown out or destroyed in other ways. How many of us have photos beyond a couple of generations back?

The rise in celebrity culture and the fixation on pregnant celebrities and their new families has provided an opportunity for observation of photographs of how some people carry in day-to-day life. Added to that, of course, are our own observations of ourselves and others around us.

Modern day

So at this point in time, people in general tend to be leading more sedentary lifestyles[9] and sitting/resting in positions that aren't good for our bodies.

Some examples include:

Hip thrusting to create a ledge

This is where we thrust our hips forwards (tipping them backwards), making an excessive curve in our lower (lumbar) spine. We're creating a resting point on our abdomen and that – plus our lower spine – bears the weight of the baby/child. Our upper body may also bear some of the weight if we're leaning backwards to allow them to rest against our chest.

Arching/rib thrusting to create a bracing area on our upper body

Here our hips may or may not be thrust forwards, depending on our tendencies. Rib thrusting is essentially leaning backwards to brace their weight on our upper body.

A reason for the common theme of passive holding may be that we tend to use passive holds more when we're standing still - and of course a lot of photographs of carrying are when people are standing still, so it's very difficult to get the full picture of baby– and child-holding throughout history. What we can do though, is work with what we've got, and also look at human biology to get an insight into how and why we carry.

If you Google "carrying a child" or "carrying child on hip" and scroll through the images that come up of in-arms carrying, you'll find plenty of examples of the carrying norm. If you study the pictures you'll find most of them are passive carrying with a tendency towards misalignment, and plenty of babies/children sitting with less-than 90 degrees angle of the hip joint (more on that later).

Observing how people carry in real life too, in non-posed carrying, the theme is similar. Although my observations come mainly from where I live, out and about, and the families I work with, I've not seen any deviation from this theme anywhere I've gone in the UK.

Although we have a limited documented history of how we carried, we thankfully don't need to rely on that to find out what the biological norm is for babies and children, and the people carrying them. In the past century there's been some great research into optimal hip angles and how babies and children naturally sit on the hip. There's also lots of information about infant reflexes, spinal development and so forth.

In this book I'll discuss carrying from both scientific and anecdotal evidence. I hope that in the future carrying will be recognised as integral to babies' development and there will be lots more carrying-related research conducted.

Baby slings and carriers

I need to point out here that while I have a passion for in-arms carrying, I do still love baby slings and carriers. They're still used in our house, and I am a babywearing trainer after all! Slings can be a vital extension of our arms, and there are some times when only a sling/carrier will work. They're fantastic tools in a parenting toolbox and can complement in-arms carrying beautifully. Let's take a little look at how slings and carrier may have helped or hindered carrying.

In recorded history, it's reasonable to draw the conclusion that slings were for the poor. They may well have been used by richer people, but drawings and paintings by English and European artists depict people living in poverty.[10] The type of carrier used in the UK varied between countries, with shawls being favoured in Wales and Scotland, and long pieces of fabric used in England.[11]

The re-emergence of a more widespread sling/carrier use in Europe since the 1970's and 1980's (with Baby Björn and Didymos playing a big role in this) has encouraged parents and carers to keep babies close, which has been wonderful for both. The reach of the babywearing community in the past decade, by online communities such as The Babywearer and Natural Mamas, sling libraries, babywearing educators, and social media, has grown exponentially. Babywearing has become much more mainstream and accessible in England, and contributes to the support and awareness of other normal parenting practices.

In England (and lots of other countries, such as the rest of the UK, various European countries, America, Canada and Australia) babywearing is used both as a practical solution to carrying on with day-to-day life whilst keeping babies calm and happy, and as a tool for bonding. With the now-widespread use of ergonomic positioning (spread-squat positioning), babywearing brings an added bonus - many babies are being carried with their legs in a similar position to how they would physiologically sit on the body

34

in-arms.

There's been some confusion over the years about newborn and young baby positioning, with babies' legs kept inside carriers until 3 months olds, and more recently the mantra "knees in line with hips" being shared far and wide. This is something I've tried to combat when training Babywearing Peer Supporters and Consultants by always coming back to "in-arms carrying is the foundation for most babywearing". If you already babywear, or are interested in doing so, you'll find lots of information throughout this book which you'll find interchangeable!

If we think about slings and carriers as tools for a specific job, rather than a tool for bonding, it would make sense that people would have used their arms more in the past. In the modern day Western world, we're in a place of privilege where babywearing is not so much a necessity for all (though it obviously is for many). Though most of us lead busy lives, many are able to find time to use babywearing as a tool for bonding.

We generally have more time on our hands through modern convenience - some more than others depending on their household's items, whether or not they need to work long hours/more than one job etc. The invention of things such as showers, hoovers, dishwashers, washing machines, cookers, microwaves and all sorts of other appliances cuts the time it takes to do things.

Babywearing can become so useful, and such a great source of closeness for parent/carer and child that babies can end up being carried in a sling/carrier for many hours each day. Babywearing can easily become a go-to way of carrying in situations where we would usually just carry in-arms – especially with the first baby you use it with!

We also have many options for baby transport, and in the UK society puts pressure on parents to treat children as miniature adults. As such, we've lost things like being used to carrying our babies and children in arms, we have little knowledge of the history of baby carrying in our culture (especially thanks to *his*tory), and are having to re-learn it all as we go along. Thankfully we still have the instinct to hold and keep our babies close.

While the abundance of options for holding our babies and children (on and off our bodies, e.g. slings, prams, bumbos, car seats) can be extremely useful, it's meant that we hold our children in arms less. Like I mentioned before, this creates repetitive cycles of holding, thinking "wow they're heavy!", and realising what other options we have, then putting them in something easier. Also, much parenting information tends to encourage parents to make sure their babies self-soothe and/or entertain themselves, which contributes to the likelihood of their babies being carried less.

This, combined with excessive use of furniture, plus more and more sedentary lifestyles, contributes to messing our bodies up, making carrying in-arms harder. Then when we're carrying in-arms we tend to adjust our bodies out of alignment to save our arms (e.g. jutting hip out to the side or hips forward to create a "shelf"). In general, we go from being flexible, aligned, strong and active individuals as young children, and gradually lose much of it. Of course there are exceptions, as well as people who are fine in one or some of these areas.

Babywearing may have contributed to us using our arms even less, but it has most definitely provided countless benefits, and for me has been the gateway to my fascination with in-arms carrying. Babywearing's benefits include a lot of the benefits of in-arms, and ergonomical positioning helps with preserving the spread-squat position, enabling babies and children to be more likely to instinctively go into it when held in arms.

Our perception of babies

If a sedentary lifestyle is normal where you live, it can also be easy to think of newborns as passive beings, especially as they need us to do so much for them. However, they are active and incredibly intelligent right from the get go. Yes, they wriggle, kick and throw their arms around, but what's happening beyond that?

Of course, we know that they aren't *really* passive beings. Parents will more often than not think that their baby is very clever, and watch them develop with fascination. Research and awareness has improved so much, that we understand a lot more about them than we used to. The problem comes from the messages we receive from society, which push the passive image and the things we're told from when we were children that seem normal.

Think again of all the devices available to hold babies in a static position, keeping them at rest. Then we're told they need things like a baby gym or baby movement classes to encourage them to move and engage. Add to that the fact - arguably largely to do with nappy companies - that most people don't know that babies are born able to communicate their need to eliminate. Then there's the push for babies to have "tummy time" each day, so they can strengthen their neck, arms and shoulders, because they spend too much time on their backs. It's all rather contradictory, isn't it?

Babies want and need to be carried, and are born ready and able to assist with this. It wouldn't make sense if they couldn't help with the carrying process, would it? So the question is, *how* do they do this, especially newborns? Well, it all begins with primitive reflexes, which I mentioned briefly earlier. We'll be looking into the different reflexes which aid carrying, and will explore how babies progress to conscious and voluntary participation.

It takes time - as with every part of their development - for them to progress through the different stages and reach their "independence" with carrying. This is the full-on clinging behaviour, just like walking and running are a result of their development of movement. If we view carrying in a similar way to their other areas of development, we can recognise the building blocks and begin understand how they fit together. As we'll discover, the carrying process is both complex and simple, and most definitely a beautiful process.

Anatomically made for carrying

So how about us - how do we fit into the carrying process? We use our arms to hold our babies and children to our bodies, but what else? Where are we likely to hold their body to? Well there are our arms again, and our hips, front, back and shoulders tend to be the other most popular places. Each of these places has their own way of making carrying possible.

People with bodies of biologically female origin tend to have wider hips. This varies in proportion from person to person, but the shape tends to be conducive to in-arms carrying, providing a convenient place for babies to sit. Babies fit to the gestational parent's hip perfectly, and adapt the width of their spread-squat position automatically, based on where they are, on the front or hip.[12] This can be seen in various positioning, as they automatically adjust to where they need to hold on to.

In evolutionary terms, the majority of gestational parents identify as female, and all gestational parents are biologically female. Non-gestational parents would have been biologically male in the vast majority of cases. When we look at in-arms carrying we need to look at the person's body's makeup. This isn't necessarily defined as "male" or "female" - it's looking at the waist-to-hip ratio (which varies hugely, even in people who identify as female), who is the primary caregiver (or person who holds the baby the most) etc.

In the most basic sense, "male" and "female" bodies have had specific roles in adult life throughout the majority of history as we know it. Men would go out and hunt, or work, and women would look after babies, children and the home. In this respect it makes a lot of sense for the differing proportions of the body based on anatomical roles such as this.

In this day and age it gets more interesting, as acknowledgement of being born in a body that doesn't represent the gender you identify as is becoming understood and more widely accepted. Also, with more and more dads being the primary caregiver, plus all-male parenting set ups too, more and more babies are being held the majority of the time by what would have been the secondary caregiver. So - in an evolutionary sense - we're moving into a new era of the traditional archetype not applying so much anymore.

So how does this translate when the evolution of humans takes so many centuries for even the slightest thing to adapt? This is a difficult one with the infancy of this understanding. An obvious thought for a person with a straighter torso wanting to hip carry would be "increase hip-to-waist ratio", but this compromises on the person's body, throwing it out of alignment, as they would need to jut their hip out. Surely there are other ways of adapting?

Funnily enough, there is a way of adapting, without actually trying to change normal carrying behaviour! Again this is coming back to the carrying reflexes and reciprocal carrying. If babies and children are born with the ability to cling, then having less of a "ledge" to hold onto surely shouldn't be too much of a problem? If so, wouldn't babies learn to work harder to hold on if their primary caregivers have a lesser waist-to-hip ratio?

This really isn't something impossible. Think about how modern-day parents in industrialised countries mostly carry passively, and over-compensate their posture and alignment to make it easier for babies/children to sit on their bodies. People who work to strengthen the clinging reflex go the opposite way. They align their bodies so hips aren't thrusting out (or at least, not so much – our spine is able to move our hips for a reason). For those with a less-significant waist-to-hip ratio this means babies hanging on with very little shelf to help.

I hypothesise that our babies are primarily designed to be carried by the bodies their biological parents possess. I say primarily, as it wouldn't make much sense if babies couldn't work with other people's shapes easily enough to be carried by different members of the community, or if they had to be cared for by someone other than their birth parents (e.g. adoption, death). From either a creation or evolutionary point of view, allowances would need to be made.

However, being designed to work well with the person/people we're most likely to be carried by (from a biological point of view) for extended periods of time would work well for both baby and caregiver.

It's been very interesting for me to observe how even within the same family my children have very different carrying "styles". This may be to do with their different experiences with in-arms carrying, but I feel like it also has to do with their own body composition and inbuilt "skill" for carrying. I think of it like any other area of development – babies and children who don't have extra limiting factors in their development will all have areas they excel in and those where they may not. This makes carrying – just like everything else – not a one-size-fits-all approach.

Clinging young

Dr. Evelin Kirkilionis described wonderfully in her book ("A Baby Wants to be Carried") how humans belong to the "clinging young" category. It was actually her mention of some of the primitive reflexes which set me on the track to a better understanding of how we're born with the ability to assist being carried.

Without rehashing what she spoke of (read her book!), here are the main characteristics of carried/clinging young:

- Grasping hands and feet

- Flexion and abduction of the legs when laying on their back, and when picked up

- Composition of breastmilk (low fat and protein), sucking speed (low) and spacing of feeds (regular/"continuous" feeders)

- Regular maternal contact

In comparison, babies who are nested/cached can have similar or different attributes.[13] For example, precocial young:

- Feed less often, with milk high in fat and protein

- Less maternal contact (adult is out searching for food for extended periods)

- Once they develop enough to follow the mother out of the nest they are able to find food for themselves

Altricial young:

- Fed more often, with low fat and protein milk

- More maternal contact

Human babies are classed as altricial young, but German biologist and behaviourist Bernhard Hassenstein felt that they didn't quite fit in it as they were carried and have clinging capabilities. He described them as "Tragling" (parent clinger, in German), and put bats, apes and marsupials in this category too.[14]

Although there's this research, and a better understanding of human behaviour, there is still a general idea in the scientific world that the grasping reflexes are no longer relevant for human carrying, and are leftover "monkey genes". Dr. Kirkilionis does agree to a certain extent of active clinging, in the sense that babies fit better on hips than anywhere else, and that babies are born knowing reflexively how to hug the hip.

I've come to see how this reflexive "hug" is a complex end-result of individual reflexes. Some of the main primitive reflexes involved in newborn carrying are:

- Palmar (hand grasp)
- Plantar (toe grasp and Babinski's sign)
- Moro (startle)
- Tonic labyrinthine (extension or flexion of body, depending on where their head is)
- Stepping (walking action)

We'll be looking into these reflexes (and more) in depth later, and at how babies can develop these reflexes into conscious holding as they grow. It makes sense that we'd be born with ways to aid the carrying process - it would be unhelpful if babies were just an inactive lump requiring extensive assistance to be held. From an evolutionary point of view it would be a major hindrance in everyday life, as well as potentially life-threatening situations.

I've a feeling this concept gets passed over because of baby slings/carriers. Though its likely carrying aids are almost as old as humans, and it's easy to get misled by the fact that they (from a basic point of view) strap the baby/child onto you, therefore don't need the baby to participate in carrying (they still can in them, but that's going off on a tangent). It's also easy to presume a number of other things, such as slings/carriers being exactly the sort we use today, and that our ancestors leading more active lives must mean they used slings a lot, when they may not.

Chapter 3

Benefits of Carrying

There are so many benefits to holding babies, with research to back it up. Babies thrive on human contact, as do adults.[1] [2] [3] In our busy lives we can end up going days or longer without meaningful human touch. If you've have a baby or child, it's much easier to get in your daily dose of human contact - in fact, many would argue it's very easy for parents to overdose on it in the early years, with the phrase "touched out" being common in parenting communities.

Positive human touch, though, is therapeutic. Although all kinds of touch can be positive or negative depending on the situation, being carried is one example of a mainly positive one. If you carry your baby in a sling/carrier they will also enjoy lots of the benefits that come from in-arms carrying!

Benefits for baby/child

The most obvious thing that comes to mind is that it's the biological norm for babies to be carried. As we've looked at already, babies were designed to be carried. They're unable to get from place to place until they can move independently on the ground, so being carried has very obvious benefits. For example, they are transported to their food source, their place of sleep, and helped with motion to soothe them.

As they're designed to be carried, they *expect* to be carried. It's inbuilt into them, wired into their very being, and it's been shown by various researchers (Bowlby, Mead, Prescott and others) that babies without regular positive human touch fail to thrive, even if they are well nourished and kept clean and healthy in other ways.

Over such a long period of time certain doctors and "parenting experts" have advocated for the separation and "independence" of babies and children, even when there is an abundance of research telling them they need the opposite. Have you ever noticed how if you can't attend to a baby's needs when they're at the stage where they really need you to, they tend to cry until you meet the need? Have you ever heard of certain cultures around the world where crying babies are a rarity? This is something easy to see as being a universal remedy, as it's proven with responsive parenting within cultures where non-responsive parenting is still advocated.[4]

Part of the problem is less understanding of the ways in which babies communicate, meaning stages of awareness are missed until the vocal cueing begins.[5] Something that contributes to missing cues is proximity to the baby, and you can't get closer than carrying. The most subtle cues can be picked up when you're holding your baby.

In-arms (or sling/carrier), babies are right there. Even if you're doing something else, the movements you feel from them alert you to what's going on. Also, verbal cues are easier to notice. This can cut out some of the stages of communication babies go through to tell you what's going on. They don't get so frustrated or upset when their needs are met in the earlier stages of communication. This encourages communication from them, and helps the parent/carer to understand the baby's needs better before they learn to speak.

So carrying also helps promote understanding of your baby/child, by you being able to pick up on other forms of communication. By being more aware of their communication, and being immediately present to respond to it, you're able to encourage them to communicate more as they know they're being heard! Better communication helps strengthen the bond between baby and parent/carer, which in turn can help the baby feel safer and more loved.

Gentle transition

Carrying also provides safety, comfort and reassurance to a baby who's gone from a nice, warm, firm, dark environment where nourishment was completely on tap, and all their needs were met instantly, to a strange new environment. Not only did they experience being born (which may have been a somewhat traumatic experience for some), they're now in a huge open space. Nothing holding them constantly, the temperature fluctuates, they experience light in a whole new way, start to feel an uncomfortable sensation in their stomach that they've not felt before (hunger) and have to learn (in their own baby way) that the people looking after you can't actually feel your hunger so they need to signal it to them.

Can you imagine the shock to the system that would be? In this scary new world they're gradually learning to adapt to, the safe, warm, comforting place is in their caregiver's arms. As a newborn they're able to scrunch up in the position they're used to on their caregiver's chest. They can take it slowly, gradually stretching out those limbs, neck and spine that have been held in the foetal position for months.

If you're thinking of using a sling, this is a perfect time to introduce it, especially ones which mimic that all-encompassing snugness such as stretchy wraps, woven wraps and ring slings. They can help ease the transition, and once they've unfurled and are more aware of what's around them, they'll be less likely to find slings and carriers restrictive.

Again, being close to a heartbeat (especially the gestational parent's) provides familiarity, which in turn can be calming.

A new point of view

As a baby becomes more alert and aware of their surroundings, at your height, babies and children get more involved in your world and the world around them. Of course, they can see the world and be aware of what's going on in many positions, including lying on their back, but up at adult height (or older child height!) gives them a different perspective and new things to look at. You may notice that they engage with you more, and interact with the world around them in new ways.

Being in-arms offers freedom of movement and the ability to look around and reach out more easily. Babywearing can help with being at a different height and communicating, but it tends to be different in-arms, especially for babies and young children. Babywearing tends to have a calming effect on babies, and some children prefer it for those times when they're tired or in a quiet mood. Carrying in-arms tends to have different dynamics. It's easier for the person carrying to move baby/child to different positions, and the differences in how they are holding on or being held can subtly (or not-so-subtly) change their interest and/or engagement.

People tend to chat more to babies who are at their level – intentionally or not. They almost become an extension of the person being spoken to, as they're attached to them. It's hard to ignore a baby or child being held, whether it's because they're trying to join in the conversation or the person talking sees them there and engages them. The baby/child benefits from communicating with new/different people as another way of exploring the world, while feeling safe in the arms of their caregiver.

There's no denying that if you're holding a baby/child, or talking to someone who is holding one, you are more aware of their presence. Babies love to imitate those around them, so are more likely to attempt to engage both you and those around you. This again helps strengthen communication skills, gives them a change of scenery, more chances to interact and practice their social skills!

Seeing what you're doing helps them to learn more - babies learn through imitation, and being at your level can pique their interest in your activity, meaning they benefit from joining in with you, and/or the extra communication when you explain what you're doing. Just watching helps them to learn about what you're doing, and the potential interaction at the same time can take that learning further. It's been shown that watching a caregiver carry out tasks stimulates the part of the brain (sensorimotor cortex) needed for babies themselves to complete the task.[6] What better point of view for observation than at adult height?

Being held can also encourage a feeling of being a part of the world around them. A sense of belonging and fulfilment is recognised as an important part of wellbeing.[7]

Being close to their caregiver's chest brings babies comfort, and can help settle them more easily, which works wonders for newborns, sleepy babies and children, and when they're ill. Being able to rest one side of their head on the caregiver's chest means they can hear their heartbeat. This is a familiar sound from the womb, so can be deeply relaxing for them. If the gestational parent is holding them, they're hearing the same heartbeat that they were used to in the womb. I remember the deeply relaxing effect of hearing my dad's heartbeat when I was snuggled up in his lap around 8 years of age, so I'd say it's great for older children too!

Being in close physical contact with someone they like/love helps strengthen their bond and improves wellbeing,[8] which is true for people of all ages – like I said earlier, positive physical contact is good for babies, children and adults alike! Positive touch can be calming, relaxing and connecting.

Being held firmly can also calm anxious babies, children and adults.[9] There are even weighted vests available to buy to try and mimic the deep pressure of a hug. This is where a fabric sling can work better in some cases than arms, as it provides a consistent, all-enveloping snugness that arms aren't always able to do. It's also why sometimes a sling is the only thing that will work for a very upset baby.

Workout for baby

In-arms carrying will help babies and children strengthen groups of muscles such as their core, while encouraging them to hold onto the parent/carer, which promotes clinging behaviour (holding on, not "being clingy"). As you'll learn throughout this book, carrying in-arms can help with a baby's physical development. Our young are born with the ability to help with the carrying process from birth through primitive reflexes, and as they get older they are able to learn to consciously cling on – even if they miss out on the transition from reflex to holding on in the early months.

Being held helps work a baby's core muscles because of the micro- and macro-adjustments they have to make to counter your movements. Muscle groups in the legs, arms and back can all be activated in different ways depending on how they're holding on. Active holding (when babies actively cling) requires babies and children to stabilise their core more than passive holding (where the carer is doing most of the work). How much work they need to do to keep balanced depends on the movements made by the person holding and the amount of participation they have in the process.

Using active carrying positions enables them to strengthen many groups of muscles, and makes carrying easier for the caregiver. Essentially, participating in active carrying is actually a whole-body exercise for the baby/child, and is (I believe) vital to optimal wellbeing. Think about all the other whole-body movements which babies and children use every single day. They come with ease, unlike to adults who tend to have to either re-learn basic movements or poorly mimic them. Rolling, squatting, crawling, cruising – all movements (and not all of them!) for your "average" 10 month old.

Carrying is part of the developmental process and is linked to so many other areas. I'll go into this more later on in the book, but for now, try to think of the carrying process just like any other area of physical development in babies and children. It has many stages, and develops and evolves over time.

Being held skin-to-skin helps regulate babies' body temperature

Another fantastic benefit of holding babies and children is how our chests are able to aid in the thermoregulation of babies and children. In non-gestational parents, biologically female people have a warmer chest temperature than biologically male people. Gestational parents' chests have a higher temperature than non-gestational parents, and lactating parents even higher![10] Thermal imaging has shown up to a whopping 3 degrees Celsius increase in lactating breasts compared to non-lactating[11] with an average of 2 degrees being recorded.[12]

Something also wonderful to know is that gestational parents' breasts are able to regulate differently on each side, meaning that you can have one baby/child skin to skin on each side and help them accordingly. [13] I find all this absolutely fascinating, and yet more proof of the amazing powers our bodies hold! This is useful in the early days and weeks when babies' own thermoregulation is underdeveloped, and when babies and children are ill. As you can see, skin-to-skin contact while moving or cuddling up can be very beneficial. This can be performed in-arms or in a sling, with in-arms being especially useful when they don't want anything around their body.

Holding your baby can help regulate their heartbeat, hormones and decrease instances of crying

It's been shown that being carried (versus being held or put in a cot) decreases heart rate and crying in babies.[14] It's also been proven that physical contact between infant and carer helps regulate hormones and emotions.[15] This again shows the incredible power of touch and the capabilities of our bodies.

Respectful in-arms carrying promotes ergonomic carrying

Ergonomic carrying, in turn, promotes good hip health. Research by Büschelberger (1961) found that the optimal position for a baby to promote hip health was a spread-squat one. He found that abduction (movement away from the mid-line – or movement away from where your leg falls straight) of 35°–40°, and flexion (bending upwards) of 90°–120° was an ideal range of positioning for the optimal development of a baby's hip joints (40° spread, 100° squat considered best) as this position evenly distributes the head of the thigh bone into the hip socket.[16] As babies grow older they show a less pronounced "M" shape when they sit on the hip – it tends to be younger babies who sit in more of a squat.

> Note: to date, no research to date shows that holding in other ways harms hip development, with the exception of tight swaddling increasing the risk of hip dysplasia. A lack of research does not mean that there aren't harmful ways of holding our babies; just that research hasn't been done in this area yet. Knowing optimal hip angles, along with knowing their unique baby, helps caregivers to decide for themselves what may be best for their situation.

When a baby is unrestricted in their movement, comfortable and happy, they will usually adopt this "classic" spread-squat position when lifted, and when held naturally to the chest or hip, even from a very young age. Some things can hinder this natural position (we'll explore this later on), and some babies have other things going on with them which interfere with being able to relax into this position.

Carrying is beneficial for babies' spines

Babies have clear stages of spinal development, but are working towards the next stage of development during their active periods. Being held in-arms provides the freedom of movement and lack of enclosed support for them to build up more muscle strength, and practice straightening the spine. The support the person carrying provides enables them to exercise safely and signal the need for rest when they tire.

The natural gentle pressure of support on the spine varies in where the arm is placed, depending on their stage of development, enabling them to work the muscles needed in different stages until the development of the spinal curves is complete.

It may help to prevent flat head syndrome

Positional flat head syndrome (plagiocephally) is a flattening of one side of the head, and is the result of babies laying on a flat surface for extended periods of time. Their skulls aren't as hard as older children and adults, and are malleable. Being held upright in-arms means there is usually no pressure on the skull, therefore can contribute to avoiding the condition if used in conjunction with other preventative measures.

When babies are carried, they may stay in the "quiet alert" state longer

For most babies, being held induces calm. When they're relaxed they are content and in an ideal state for learning. This is to do with having all their needs met and being in a place of safety and comfort. More time spent in the "quiet alert" state means more time in the optimal state for learning and developing.

May reduce the need for "tummy time"

Whilst the idea of "tummy time" is controversial, it's worth mentioning here as the ideas behind it link in well to carrying. "Tummy time" was introduced following the implementation of the "back to sleep" program (sleeping babies on their backs instead of fronts to improve SIDS rates). With the huge reduction in time spent on their tummies, concerns were raised about flat head syndrome and under-use of muscles stimulated whilst on their front. "Tummy time" was introduced to encourage time spent off their backs and as exercise for very young babies.

The seemingly biggest issue many parents run into with "tummy time" is that not many babies seem to like it. This makes a lot of sense, as the muscles needed to comfortably enjoy time on their tummies are very much underdeveloped at such a young age. You may have experienced yourself the upset of witnessing your baby keep dropping their head to the ground as they battle to hold themselves up or the cries of pain from a baby who has digestive issues.

Thankfully there's been research conducted which shows no difference between babies meeting milestones from before the "back to sleep" campaign and since "tummy time" was introduced.[17] Also, before "tummy time", babies were sleeping on their front, not exercising in their sleep!

So how does this relate to carrying? Well, being held upright in-arms provides babies with a chance to make the micro– and macro-adjustments babies and children have to make to compensate for your movement. This engages their core muscles, encourages the development of head and upper body control and helps with vestibular (balance) development. They're also off their backs so their skull isn't experiencing any pressure.

Carrying is good exercise

We know that walking is a cardiovascular exercise that is very good for our health. Really, it's essential for our health – movement is part of our very survival. Walking at a relaxed pace is classed as low intensity steady state (LISS) exercise.

Adding the weight of our baby/child to our walks can be beneficial, especially if we make sure we're holding our bodies in alignment and our posture is good. Carrying in a sling uses more calories than not carrying, as you've increased the load your body needs to move, so using a carrier can be a good form of exercise. While walking with an extra load, our bodies work harder, our heart rate increase, and our metabolic rate is increased. When holding around our centre of mass, or a bit higher up (think between backpack height and around your midsection), we see an increase in energy expenditure that correlates directly to the weight we're carrying.[18] This means that a 150lb person holding a 15lb baby in a sling (10% of bodyweight) would see a 10% increase in metabolic rate at the time.

However, it's been found that when you carry in-arms you may burn up to 16% more calories than when using a carrying aid. Not only that, it may even burn more calories than breastfeeding.[19] This is because you're using more muscle groups and moving them around from time to time. So, carrying may also aid weight loss - in conjunction with a healthy diet, of course. If you carry a lot and want to maintain your weight, you'll get to eat a bit more to counteract the calorie deficit from all that exercise! It's a great way to exercise and move more, whilst bonding with your baby/child. As I'll speak about later, carrying in-arms provides you with a whole-body workout, as well as your baby/child!

Carrying can also build up overall strength as well as endurance

I find it fascinating, how incredibly well designed we are as humans. Our babies are born relatively light in weight, even if they're on the heavier end of "normal". Then, they gradually gain weight over the weeks, months and years as they develop physically. They get heavier as they are able to move around more, and we gradually hold them less as they are able to explore their environment day to day, and learn to walk greater distances when out and about.

The gestational parent even gets a head-start on carrying while they're pregnant. Once the baby or babies are born, the "bump" just shifts upwards to their chest (minus the extra weight from the waters, extra blood, placenta etc.). As the baby grows, our muscles get used to that slowly increasing weight and strengthen in line with it. The more the baby is carried, the more our endurance is built up, and (when done correctly) you're able to carry comfortably for long periods of time.

Carrying can save time

I don't know about you, but meeting everyone's needs as efficiently as possible is high up on my parenting list most of the time. When there's both my husband and me around I have more time to focus on each person, but when I'm parenting alone, I need all the "shortcuts" I can get. Like I mentioned previously, carrying cuts out a lot of hassle. It cuts down how many stages of communication my baby needs to cycle through to get me to hear him, and I know that even if he needs something other than being held, the simple act of close contact means he'll (most likely) be content for a bit longer, as long as I got to him quick enough.

A quick up in-arms helps me meet either person's needs without antagonising one, both or more. Sometimes I may need both hands, and if he's willing to be carried in the sling then that's brilliant. Keeping stress levels lower for me and the others is important.

Communication and interaction

I mentioned before about how carrying facilitates communication and interaction. From a personal point of view, something I've found with all of my children is how they engage with me more when they're carried. Being up at an adult's level provides a whole new view, more opportunities to learn, and surely makes life that bit more exciting!

What's been interesting is how they interact *even more* when in-arms. Things like freedom of movement, being able to turn their whole body and the way they can instigate you changing their position (and therefore their viewing/interaction angle) all help them to enhance their carrying experience.

Again, cues are also much easier to read when they're carried. Like I said, either a sling/carrier or in-arms, but there can be less room for confusion in-arms with more active cues. For example, asking for milk in a sling is a more frustrated and frantic one for Isaac as he's held so close. I can confuse it for needing a wee, until he's out of the sling and can tell me properly.

Observing the thousands of babies and their caregivers who I've worked with over the past 5 years has taught me so much about human behaviour. Looking out for these behaviours in society around me has shown many correlations and given me an itch to learn more about how babies communicate and how in-arms carrying facilitates this, and I hope that one day more research will be done about these subjects.

Babies communicate in so many verbal and non-verbal ways, but on the body, it's unmistakeable that these communications get picked up earlier. This helps caregivers respond to the baby sooner, minimising them going past the active alert stage where non-stressed communication of a need takes place.

I like to think of it as similar to sending a text versus talking on a telephone, and video call as opposed to talking face to face. In all scenarios information is being shared. The difference is how much information you receive, and it's not all about the words being used. Take, for example, someone may text you "Help!". This could be interpreted in several ways. Three examples could be: an emergency, "get me out of here" or "I have a problem". Now, on the telephone you would hear the tone of their voice and may be able to distinguish better between an emergency, wanting you to save them from a boring conversation or needing help with a problem. Video call works even better, with having voice plus facial expression – you get even more of the situation from these non-verbal clues.

Yet when face to face you get *so* much more of the story. Nothing grabs your attention quite the same as someone being right in your face! Not only that, there are the 3 dimensional aspects. The person is sharing your space rather than being behind a screen. Everything is 3 dimensional – on a screen things can be very 2 dimensional and you may get the gist but not the whole story. The subtle nuances, the sounds you hear closer up, the things you see in real life, not separated by a screen.

When held, babies and children tend to be more physical with their communication. They communicate more with their bodies and hands – everything is that bit more tactile, from a hand on your cheek, pulling your face to look somewhere, to a kiss out of nowhere.

Physical interaction with the world around them can be easier as they are higher up, able to move in an upright position and can physically and/or verbally communicate to their caregiver that they want to touch something.

If you carry your baby in a sling or carrier, have you come across times when your baby is getting antsy, ends up distressed and the only thing that calms them is the sling/carrier? For me and so many others it's another (bloody amazing!) tool in our parenting toolkit that we know has an "if all else fails….." kind of magic. I used to wonder why a sling would work when my arms wouldn't, but I've got a different perspective now.

The snugness, all-encompassing hold of the sling creates a calm, stress-relieving environment. Much like how older children and adults can be calmed by firm, loving holding. In a relaxation-inducing environment, it makes sense that it's more conducive to calming and helping them chill out (hands up, how many of you have popped a sling/carrier around your baby and had them zonk out faster than the speed of light?) This isn't a bad thing at all - just like everything, each thing has its stronger points.

While carrying in-arms can definitely relax a baby/child and help them sleep, for many a sling/carrier does the job better. And so with communication, both happen in each situation, but it can be easier to communicate in-arms than in a sling.

A note on safety

While there are several potential safety concerns when carrying, many have no scientific backing. This is not to say they aren't valid, just that they require further investigation before being "proven". There are 3 main safety considerations when it comes to in-arms carrying.

Safety considerations

Chin off chest

Before babies are able to fully support their head and neck it's very important to keep an eye on how close their chin is to their chest. Their chin needs to be at least 2cm away from their chest to keep their airways unrestricted. Very young babies have narrow airways so are more easily restricted.

For older babies and children, greater awareness is needed when they're asleep, again due to the lack of neck control.

Fall hazards

Being cognizant of how your baby/child is behaving will reduce the risk of falling. If they're restless and are making random movements/flinging themselves around, it's probably not the best idea to keep carrying them.

Spatial awareness

Awareness of your environment and your baby/child is important. Being mindful of what's in and around yours and their personal space will help you to avoid bumps and trips.

Chapter 4

Physiology of Babies

To understand how best to carry babies and children, it's helpful to learn about how they develop and what their specific needs are at different stages of development. Here we will look at the normal physical development of babies as they relate to carrying.

Stages of Spinal Development

When you're carrying, it's important to support the baby's spinal development. This means remembering where they are in their physical development and respecting their need for both active and passive carrying. The spine is an incredibly complex part of our body, having many more uses than just helping keep us upright. Encouraging normal spinal development and normal bodily movements will help keep the body aligned and strong as children grow.

Babies are born with a "C" shaped spine. In a child with no spinal issues, it develops gradually into a "J" shape as they progress through sitting, crawling to walking. Depending on environmental factors, the spine will either stay closer to this "J" shape or develop into a more pronounced "S" shape as the baby grows from child to adult. We'll look at environmental factors which affect the spine later on in the book.

If we look at the spinal development from a point of view that the process happens not as one thing at a time, but with lots of overlaps, it's easier to understand how to support their development without just focusing on one area at a time. I'll discuss the different spinal curves as relative to a single stage, but we'll explore the overlaps after this.

So, the first curve to reach full development is the cervical (neck) one. It begins to develop as soon as they're born, as they're held upright. Development increases as baby starts to engage with the world, look around, follows lights and sounds etc., and is completed when baby is able to fully support their head and neck. The age at which this happens is dependent on how developed these muscles are already (babies vary greatly in their strength from birth) and what opportunities are provided for their stimulation.

As a species whose young is reliant on the caregiver/s to get them from A to B, and who are designed to be carried, it makes sense that being carried would help with the development of the muscles needed for independence, doesn't it? To support the developing neck, we need to allow baby the freedom of movement when they want to look around, and support their head and/or neck when they tire or are asleep.

The next spinal curve to complete is the thoracic curve. As they learn to sit up, the muscles in the upper and middle spine get stronger and the spinal region here starts straightening out. How do babies learn to sit? Sitting can seem to appear out of nowhere, when you realise they're getting very good at controlling their trunk. People tend to test out whether their baby can sit, and when they are able to aid themselves by using their hands to prop themselves up it becomes a regular practice until they can sit completely unaided.

Carrying is part of the process of development to sitting unaided, as they are essentially "sitting" on your body, aided. By allowing the freedom of movement, exercise of the muscles and practice of straightening the spine during carrying you're actively supporting their development towards sitting unaided.

In carrying, support for the lower spine and/or bum with little or no upper body support (depending on development) can aid in the upper body's development. Freedom of movement and the opportunities to stabilise their upper body exercises the muscles used in holding their body up when sitting.

When babies begin to crawl the lumbar (lower back) curve develops, and is complete when they are able to walk unaided. As they've mastered sitting and upper body strength and control, they can now focus on the lower half of their body and build up more strength in their legs. Crawling leads to pulling up to stand, then a supported squat, then cruising, standing, unsupported squat, and – finally – walking.

During this process of development, babies also gradually take control over the clinging action when they're carried. Reflexive leg positioning becomes conscious positioning, and so begins the development to full-body voluntary clinging.

It is also optimal for the baby/child to be supported with their spine in that gentle "C" position - or an upside down question mark for a better visual - when they are tired or they are asleep. This foetal tuck-type position allows your baby/child to rest in a way that reduces the pressure on the spine and hips.

How a baby sits on you is obviously dependent on their developmental progress, as well as whether they are alert and active, or tired and wanting to rest. Here are some visuals which, whilst not anatomically correct, give a better understanding of what's happening with their spine at different stages.

Babies in the "C" position

When babies are beginning to develop the first curve in their spine, they tend to sit like an upside down question mark. Their neck is straighter (chin off chest), and the rest of the spine is curved. Even when they're asleep, we keep their chin off their chest so the spine doesn't revert back into a complete "C". This is also an at-rest position that babies go into, and children also, although less pronounced.

When babies are sitting actively on a caregiver, they tend to sit in a "J" position. Even very young babies adopt variations of this straightened spine when active, and also when in a sling. Even newborns tend to sit in more active positions with a straighter back when awake. This is because the spine doesn't just suddenly straighten out or gain a curve out of the blue. A combination of muscular development and regular straightening enables this over a process of weeks and months.

Babies in the "J" position

When you think about the stages of spinal development it can be disconcerting to see a baby sitting up so straight, and you may feel the need to try and encourage them back into the question mark shape. In actual fact this is completely normal positioning. Again, babies practice straightening out and spinal development stages overlap - no stage appears out of the blue.

They practice straightening out when they're put to sleep on their backs, when they're put down for a nappy change, when they're put in a car seat or pram and so forth. The straightening out in-arms (or sling) is also normal – we just need to keep aware of their tired cues so we can support them back in the question mark shape once they've had enough.

A concern is the amount of pressure put on a baby's spine during the developmental process. Babies are put on their backs from birth, especially for sleeping. When a baby's nappy is changed, their legs tend to be lifted up, putting pressure on the upper– and mid-back, instead of rolling them onto their side. Car seats and prams also put babies into a flat position. Excessive time on the back can cause the skull to flatten at the back (plagiocephaly or flat head syndrome), which we can see, so think about what's happening with the spine, which we can't see. Babies' bones are softer than adults, and are malleable.

Some babies are also put in things like bumbos, jumperoos and baby walkers, being put into positions they're not ready for developmentally. This makes them bear weight in places where they're not muscularly developed enough yet to do so without creating undue spinal pressure.

So how do we support spinal development and avoid undue spinal pressure when carrying? Well, to start with, we can observe where the baby is at developmentally. This gives us a snapshot of how the spine has developed so far, what stage they're working towards and how close they are to it. This enables us to work out what support they need and where.

For example, a baby who is moving towards full head and neck control needs varying degrees of support from the neck downwards when carried. Sometimes they won't need neck support, as they'll be practicing holding their head up. Like I mentioned earlier, spinal development is overlapping as the baby works towards the next stage of completion. A hand on the upper back while they sit on the forearm of your other arm, or full support from one arm, works well to keep them steady.

A baby with good neck control will need support from the upper back downwards, as they gain the upper body strength required to hold themselves up sitting unaided. When active, they'll be able to spend more and more time with no upper back support as they practice balancing and controlling their torso. This is where the focus is on support for the lower spine and body, gradually allowing them more practice for the lower spine also.

Once sitting unaided, the main focus shifts to building up overall strength. At this stage, swapping between gentle supporting of the upper– and lower-back is natural, and changes where the baby/child needs to work to support themselves or hold on.

So we know that babies need spinal support as they develop the strength to support their bodies independently. We also know that extended periods of time in containers or on their backs isn't recommended, and that pressure points should be avoided, so how can we provide this support without creating negative pressure points from our support.

Well, for a start, the pressure from a hand or forearm is different to being laid down on a flat surface, sitting in a car seat or similar, or pressure being applied, for example, by a knot tied at the back or under the bum of a baby in a sling. Our bodies aren't a manmade invention. Our make up is compatible with other humans, and we know how cleverly our bodies have been designed to transport our young. Of course, this doesn't mean that we can't make errors in *how* we use our bodies, but it does mean that we're working with materials designed to be used for carrying.

The support from a hand or arm produces only enough pressure for a baby to steady themselves against, and isn't a squeezing or pressing action. A forearm to sit on generally provides a place for the upper thighs to sit on with the bum hanging over to a certain degree. A hand supporting a newborn's bum is gentler than sitting in a car seat.

Hip development

Healthy hips are important for many reasons, including the fact they help move our legs when walking, enable us to perform squatting movements and are connected to other parts of our body. Our hip flexor muscles connect our thighs with our lumbar spine and pelvis. A healthy range of motion and strength in the hips help to protect our knees and lower back. If these muscles are weak they can lead to postural problems which cause other parts of the body to work harder, leading to a higher risk of injury.

As you can imagine, it's important that we encourage good hip health at all ages. So how can we do this with babies? You've probably guessed already, but carrying can play an important role in promoting healthy hips.

It's really interesting to look at the different medical and research viewpoints on optimal hip positioning. As we saw previously, there is evidence to show that abduction (movement away from the mid-line) of 35°–40°, and flexion (bending) of 90°–120° is considered the ideal range of positioning for the optimal development of a baby's hip joints (40° spread, 100° squat considered best). This position evenly distributes the head of the thigh bone into the hip socket.[1]

When babies are born they still have a lot of cartilage which needs to harden (ossify) into bone. Hip sockets are one such area of cartilage, and hips regularly held in this optimal angle enable the sockets (acetabulum) to ossify around the head of the thigh bone correctly. Ossification of the hip socket happens throughout 3-9 months of age.[2]

Whilst there isn't any research showing that babies not regularly held in this position will come to harm, it has been shown that the fact that babies have tight iliopsoas muscle makes them more vulnerable to passive extension.[3] It seems more research needs to be conducted into the differences between babies and children who are carried in this spread-squat position and those who aren't to find out if there are any health implications.

You may have heard the term "hip dysplasia". This is where the socket of the hip is too shallow and the femoral head of the thigh bone doesn't sit in it correctly. It can sometimes result in dislocation, but is very rare. In the UK there's an incidence of developmental dysplasia of the hip (DDH) which needs treatment in 1-2 in every 1000 live births.[4]

A common treatment for this is using a pavlik harness, which holds babies legs in an "m" position, spread at 30-45 degrees and squat at 90-110 degrees. This is within the normal range of motion babies sit on us in a spread-squat position. In fact, Dr. Kirkilionis is passionate about asking parents to consider using carrying as a form of treatment because the rate of recovery without the use of devices or other treatment is as high as 60-80%,[5] and she feels babies are being affected negatively in other ways by having their movement restricted.[6]

An interesting insight is that carrying on the front of the body tends to be a more passive position than hip carrying, and babies usually end up sitting in a chair-like position (hips at 90 degrees) and at times with the hips in a sub-90 degree angle. This happens from birth. With the sub-90 degree angle, some of this tends to be to do with misplacement of positioning (especially with very young babies) but sometimes it's just how a baby wants to sit. A relaxed or alert newborn baby will usually sit with their hips at a 90 degree or higher angle squat position. If the angle is less than this, it's usually found when a baby is uncomfortable or distressed, or in hypertonic babies.

As babies tend to be carried mainly on the front in-arms for most of the first half year of their lives, this leads me to believe that different positions have their own place in babies' health and development, as a normal range of motion for babies to include in their daily movement repertoire. Normal carrying on the front supports the research showing a 90 degree sitting angle or higher is optimal for hip health, so there is no rush to move a baby onto the hip before it feels comfortable for you. Some dyads are ready for hip carrying as early as 3 months or even less, and some later than 6 months. There's no right or wrong age to start hip carrying, as long as you follow your baby's cues, development, and how it feels for you too.

Foetal tuck

The foetal tuck is the scrunched up, frog-like position very young babies are associated with. It's most prominent in the first 14 days after the birth of a "term" baby, and why photographers prefer doing newborn shoots before 2 weeks of age (all those scrunched up and posed shots are much easier then!). It's the position they stay in the most, and it's no wonder, seeing as they've been held in it by the womb for many months before they were born! It takes time for them to adapt to their new environment and for their muscles, ligaments and tendons to stretch out.

After this point they really begin unfurling and stretching out more. This position conserves the most energy, decreases the surface area of the body (so keeps them warmer) and is a natural position of rest. It's no wonder that close variations of this position babies and children revert back to (or we adjust their position to) when they fall asleep in-arms or in a sling/carrier. As the muscles relax, the body naturally curves inward.

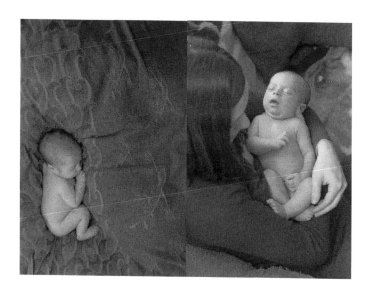

Isaac, 13 days old

In the foetal tuck, the hips tend to be less open, and the knees higher up on the body. Legs may be crossed or uncrossed, and knees may be so high up that the feet "disappear". The range of movement increases over time, and the muscles and tendons of the hips and knees allow for progression to the spread-squat position shown when a baby is held to the hip.

It's when babies are in this position that they tend to suffer the most manipulation in slings and carriers, to try to reach an "ideal" picture of positioning (knees in line with hips, legs parallel, but still in a nice squat), rather than taking cues from their natural in-arms position and tying the sling/carrier around that.[7]

Spread-squat position

The spread-squat position is human babies' natural clinging

stance and their behaviour in this position enables them to be carried with ease. Different reflexes trigger babies to go into this position before they're consciously able to choose to.

As the ligaments of the hips and knees become less tight babies are able to gradually move into a wider spread-squat stance, going from this to this:

Legs angled inwards to legs angled outwards

The spread-squat also enables the optimal hip positioning noted earlier, and is found throughout many stages of babies' development – not just in carrying. As previously mentioned, it is also the position used in the treatment of DDH.

Younger babies tend to sit in a deeper squat than older babies and children during active carrying, and my theory is that it's because it requires more work to consciously hold on in a deeper squat, once the reflexes have integrated. The deeper squat prevails throughout the reflexive carrying phase, and becomes shallower as they transition to voluntary clinging. They then vary their squat depth depending on what part of their body is doing the most work, or how much work you are doing for them.

Muscular development

Babies' muscles develop over the course of weeks and months (along with the spine) to enable them to move from one place to another unaided, support the weight of their body and eventually walk. Completion of spinal development is sequential from the neck down to the base of the spine, and muscular development correlates with this.

There are around 640 muscles in the body, and it's the skeletal ones that we're interested in when it comes to carrying. These muscles are voluntary ones, meaning we can control what they do (unlike smooth muscles, which are involuntary). Tendons connect muscles and bones, and move along with them. Babies are born with an underdeveloped musculoskeletal system, and it takes many months for this to mature. Movement is essential for the development of muscles and for good health at all ages. Babies and children need freedom of movement to develop and maintain strength and by also giving them this through carrying in-arms it allows for normal development.

Common muscle groups used in clinging

Arms

When an arm is hooked around the carers to hold on, the biceps, triceps and forearm are activated. Sometimes the hand may be used too.

Torso

The abdominal muscles are used to stabilise the baby/child against the movements you make as you walk. Muscles in the back are also activated.

Legs

Depending on where you are supporting them, the muscles in their thighs and/or calves are used to hold on. The feet are also used in some positions.

Carrying in active positions encourages a wide range of muscular development all over the body. Depending on the position they're being held in, and how active or passive the position is for them, different muscle groups are activated.

The repetition of movements over and over again over the course of weeks and months strengthen their muscles, and their ever-increasing bodyweight adds more resistance, strengthening them further. That, in addition to requiring less and less support, enables a continual progression of getting stronger and able to balance better. As they grow, they become less "top heavy" with their heads being more in proportion with the rest of their body, which also aids balance.

Just as the progression through to walking takes many months, the progression through to fully independent clinging does also. In fact, it takes even longer! We see the stages babies go through with their movement to reach independence, and we see the same with different stages of carrying.

> Something fun to try with a bigger baby (one who has full torso control) is to place your hand on their tummy when you're holding them in-arms, walk normally and then make various movements. You should be able to feel their abdominal muscles contract to counter your movement and keep them stable.

Central Nervous System

The central nervous system (CNS) is made up of the brainstem and spinal cord. Reflex movements occur via spinal cord pathways and neurons are how different parts of the body communicate with each other via the brain and the spinal cord. Our genes and the environment we're in both contribute to the development of the CNS.

Development of the CNS begins in utero and continues long after birth, completing in adulthood. There are huge changes in the brain in the first year of life, and the cerebellum triples in size, which is thought to be related to the rapid development of motor skills.

As environmental factors and experiences have a great ability to affect brain development, babies and children are especially vulnerable to negative experiences. This is why it's important to encourage normal development by enabling them to perform the repetitive actions required to integrate primitive reflexes and develop gross motor skills. In time perceptual-motor development (receiving a sensory input and moving accordingly) will enable the baby to willingly participate in carrying.

"Tummy time"

Let's revisit "tummy time" again briefly. As we know, experts believed that if parents gave their babies regular "tummy time" then it would help build their upper body strength, by exercising their neck, shoulders and arms, enabling them to reach milestones such as reaching, rolling over, and crawling. We also know that the age of reaching such milestones hasn't changed since before "tummy time" was introduced.

The advice is to have them engage in "tummy time" several times a day from days old and increasing the period of time as they get older and stronger. It's definitely true that muscles are engaged in different ways in different positions, but in the early days when they have so little strength to hold themselves up, is it truly necessary? Kind of like babies don't need to be sat up unaided when they can't physically do so to be able to eventually do so. There are other ways of gaining strength until they're able to try more comfortably by themselves.

However, I completely agree that babies need to spend less time on their backs and in "containers", but why has carrying been overlooked here? Carrying enables them to strengthen their neck muscles, core muscles, leg muscles, to balance themselves, as well as having many other benefits that we've already covered (and undoubtedly many more!). This is yet another way that carrying as a developmental process is not being recognised.

Communication

Babies communicate in so many different ways, and this deserves a whole book on the subject! Here we'll explore how babies communicate in relation to the carrying process, and how that communication progresses as they develop.

In the early days and weeks communication is instinctive or reflexive, much like the primitive reflexes we'll look at in the next chapter. Babies use interesting ways of communicating, including wriggling, kicking, facial expressions and vocalisations. In carrying, paying attention to the 7 stages of awareness can help with recognising and responding to their communication.[8] Babies will use subtle and not-so-subtle movements to signal a need for a change of position, or to communicate something unrelated to carrying.

Parts of the body used when clinging

Clinging when carrying can be a whole-body action. Depending on the hold being used, different parts of the body and different muscle groups are engaged. For example, muscles in the thigh, calves and feet may all activated when using active carries on the hip, as well as the core muscles (those in the torso – not just their abs) and usually an arm too. Their necks also need to keep stabilised from the motion. An active shoulder carry though would see much less activation of the leg muscles as it's the upper body doing most of the work.

Now, let's take a look at newborn carrying, and how it lays the foundation for clinging behaviour.

Chapter 5

Primitive Reflexes

In this chapter we're going to look at some primitive reflexes and explore how they relate to in-arms carrying. The **in-arms carrying online course** goes into more detail, and uses videos to see these in action.

Babies are born with a host of reflexes. Some reflexes we're born with won't go (for example, breathing, sneezing etc.), but others will integrate at varying ages (some as early as a couple of months, others as late as 12 months or more). The primitive reflexes are replaced by postural reflexes and voluntary actions, which remain for life.

Postural reflexes are to do with balance, coordination and motor development, and our brains can override them if need be. For example, the reflexive response to pain is to flinch away from it, but if you want to walk over hot coals (or barefoot on a hot path), you can make your body do it.

Primitive reflexes come from the lower brain (brain stem), and integrate as the nervous system matures and the muscles and spine are able to bear the load and duration of voluntary movements. Basically, a movement is implemented from the spinal cord (each vertebra is relevant to different parts of the body, and damage to any of them can result in loss of function to the corresponding area and nerves) and triggers muscular activation in the relevant area. Each reflex requires activation by a relevant trigger, which sets off a sequence of involuntary movement.

If any primitive reflexes are retained, they can cause

developmental delays and issues such as lack of concentration, sleep issues, and troubles with balance and coordination. It's also common for people with autism[1], learning difficulties[2] or ADHD[3] to have retained primitive reflexes.

Lots of things can cause reflexes to be retained, and it can happen as early as birth. How baby was born, whether the birth was traumatic, head trauma etc. can all lead to retained reflexes. Accidents, skipping developmental stages or not spending enough time in them, illness, overuse of baby "containers" and lack of the repetitive movements babies make are also risk factors.

The retention of reflexes can lead to difficulties for the child as they get older, including into adulthood. It is possible to integrate them with certain movement/exercise programs designed specifically for retained reflexes, and there are some great resources and books on this subject.[4]

Normal reflex integration

Reflexes integrate when babies are given the opportunity to make the repetitive movements associated with each reflex. This means exploring their environment, not being kept in one position/contained for long periods of time, and their carers doing things they normally would with a baby to encourage their development.

As I noted above, skipping developmental stages or staying at a stage for too short a time can prevent integration of certain reflexes. This could be a baby going from sitting to walking, missing the crawling stage, or not spending enough time practicing grasping, for example. For some reason carrying isn't seen as a developmental process, but it surely is.

Why are we born with primitive reflexes?

As human babies have an underdeveloped musculoskeletal system, we're born with certain reflex actions. Having reflexes helps us to do certain things before our bodies are strong enough to, or before we're able to them consciously. The rooting and sucking reflexes, for example, enable us to search out and consume milk before we're consciously aware of where it comes from and how we suck.

Others, like the spinal galant reflex, enable babies to navigate the birth canal. This reflex is triggered when the skin along the side of a baby's back is stroked. The reaction is that the baby will swing towards the side that was stroked, and this helps with the birthing process.

There are some reflexes that may seem to have no real use for newborns at first glance, such as the palmar and plantar reflexes. The palmar reflex is the automatic grasping action that happens when you put your finger (or an object) in a newborn's hand. The plantar reflexes are the flexion of the toes when pressure is put on the ball of the foot, and an extension and fanning of the toes when the foot is stroked. The common explanation for these reflexes is that they're leftover from "when we had fur", and that they serve no purpose these days as we don't hold onto body hair to get around.

On the postural side of things, it takes many weeks and months to build up the strength needed, and for our spine to develop the curves needed to do things like constantly hold our head up, sit unaided, crawl and walk.

Primitive reflexes fill in the gaps and I find them absolutely fascinating. Some are active from different stages in utero and others from birth. When you think about how babies drink the amniotic fluid, play with their cord and somehow manage to manipulate their bodies to get out of the birth canal, it's clear that reflexes play an important role in both development and survival. This is why I don't believe any of the primitive reflexes are evolution's "leftovers".

I believe that some reflexes may seem pointless simply because our "normal" is so far from what actually is biologically normal these days. Things get overlooked, or attributed to something else simply because we're not looking at the whole picture. When you dig below the surface of these reflexes, the bigger picture that's painted by the layers and nuances is downright incredible. It's something which creates a new awareness of the complexity of the seemingly simplest of things, and I hope you will find them as fascinating as I do!

As we explore some of the primitive reflexes you'll notice a theme. We'll think about what their uses are commonly believed to be for, as well as how they might work in other scenarios. While there's still truth to much of the common beliefs, thinking about them from another angle opens up new thoughts and ideas that align with the concept of these reflexes being linked to carrying as well.

Why don't we know much about carrying reflexes?

I love this acronym that I first heard of from Katy Bowman— WEIRD.[5] I'm going to come back to Katy in a moment, as she talks a lot of sense!

WEIRD means: Western, Educated, Industrialized, Rich and Democratic. It stems from participants in psychological studies but I think it also describes very well the typical idea of what is right, progressive or normal in other areas of Western life. In an effort to be more and more "advanced", we're so far from what normal actually is, and we're paying the price with our health.

So, WEIRD is what people tend to base our current "normal" on. For example, recommendations for how much exercise we should take part in each week is coming from a drive to get people more active, and using this umbrella term "exercise" for doing set activities rather than tackling the root of the problem – we need to move more in our everyday lives to stay healthy as a whole. It's like a dentist filling a cavity but not giving instruction on how to keep your teeth healthy to prevent another from happening.

In comparison, that "latent monkey genes" idea is out there because carrying isn't thought of as a developmental process. So little thought is given to carrying as a part of normal development that things get overlooked. Things are explained away instead of exploring further.

Recorded research into infant reflexes started at a time when mothers (or gestational parents) were the definitive primary carers of babies. Doctors and researchers were primarily men, who of course didn't have the same lived experience and understanding as the people raising babies and children.

I believe this is where the hypothesis for the "non-essential" (e.g. non life-sustaining) infant reflexes comes from. Basically, if you don't know what you're looking for, you're not going to get the whole picture, are you? And if you have pre-conceived notions of what humans should or shouldn't do, and believe in evolution, then you're going to see and interpret things differently.

So, with this in mind, let's go back to Katy. With her work in the biomechanical field, she talks about how research is conducted with a skewed belief of what "normal" is. "Normal" is how the majority of people behave, the diet the majority eat, the way the majority of bodies are, the way our normal environments affect our development.

Think about this in terms of carrying/not carrying. "Normal" was and is using prams to get babies around. Normal is holding babies and children in passive positions, shifting our bodies out of alignment for more leverage, thinking they're too heavy, using devices regularly which mean we don't need to use our arms. It's no wonder that research isn't coming from a *true* definition of normal, of what is biologically normal! Research is coming from the mindset of young babies being fairly passive beings, and any sort of active responses that don't relate to breathing and eating must be either latent "monkey genes" or to do with a later stage of development. Again, carrying as a developmental process just isn't a "thing".

So, let's throw that all out of the window and look at the following reflexes from the point of view that babies are inherently active and intelligent beings, unconsciously through to consciously able to participate in carrying. Let's also come from an angle that carrying is an important part of the development of the musculoskeletal system, and links into other developmental areas, and see what comes up.

Palmar reflex

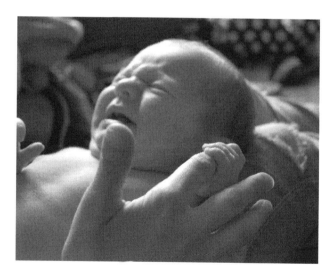

Palmar grasp

The palmar grasp is triggered when an object is pressed or stroked on the baby's palm. The response elicited is the tight closure of the hand and the grasp is so strong that babies are able to support their entire bodyweight if they were to be held hanging!

This reflex begins to integrate as babies' motor development advances to the stage of consciously reaching for and grasping objects. Caregivers are usually encouraged to help this developmental process by placing small toys in the baby's hand when they become more aware of their surroundings.

It's generally thought to be a "leftover" reflex in evolutionary terms, in that it would have been used for babies to cling on to their mother's body hair. I feel that using this as a comparison is unhelpful as it leads us away from exploring its uses and potential today.

In carrying today, it still has a purpose. Maybe you've witnessed or experienced one or more of the following examples? Have you noticed how babies who haven't yet integrated this reflex have a tendency to grab onto any hair, clothing or anything graspable that brushes their hands? Have you ever tried to pry a tiny clenched fist open to get them to let go? (You can release this grip by stroking the little finger side of their hand).

The plantar grasp helps steady a wobbly baby, keeping them secure. That frustrating vice-like grip is a survival instinct and enables them to hold on, keeping them safe. It will sometimes be seen along with the Moro reflex, as a clinging instinct either after or at the end of the reflex.

Upper extremity proprioceptive placing

This is a reflex which helps stabilise a baby when their upper body control is still weak. When the top of the hand is rubbed, the response is that the arm flexes, lifts up and the hand "places" itself. It's usually tested by rubbing the hand on the underside of a desk, so that the baby will then place its hand on the top of the desk.

Plantar reflexes

Babinski's sign

This plantar reflex happens when the sole or sides of the foot are stroked, and presents as an extension of the big toe, and may also be accompanied by a fanning of the toes.

It's one of the longest appearing reflexes, this starts integrating as the toddler becomes stable and balanced in their walking. It helps by widening the width of the toe area, which helps to stabilise them as they stand, climb and walk.

It's a reflex that at first glance appears to not serve a purpose in the early days, but if we think about how it presents in carrying, this reflex helps stabilise the baby when their foot slips on the person carrying's body. It tends to go hand-in-hand with the next reflex, the plantar grasp.

Plantar grasp

This reflex is elicited by pressure to the ball of the foot and manifests as a clenching of the toes.

This is another reflex thought to be a leftover one, used for clinging onto the caregiver's body hair, but in carrying it's a way for the baby to grip onto clothing or skin as they stabilise themselves. So it's not used in quite the same way as other primates, in that it's not used to hold on for any length of time, but is most definitely a carrying reflex.

This is another reflex commonly seen alongside the Moro reflex, helping with clinging and staying secure.

Tonic labyrinthine reflex

The tonic labyrinthine reflex is to do with balance and muscle tone. It's present up to around 4 months old, and begins around 3 months after conception. It's responsible for the foetal tuck position that babies adopt in the womb.

TLR extension (head behind midline)

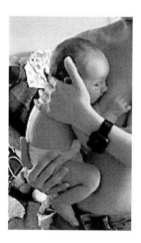

TLR flexion (head in front of midline)

When the head is in front of the midline of the body (imagine an invisible line going down through the crown of their head), the reflex action is a flexion of the limbs and the spine curves inward. In carrying, this promotes the physiological carrying position. When the head is behind the midline of the body, the response is an extension/straightening of the body and limbs, or the just the spine, depending on the position they're in (in carrying the legs tend to keep up in the squat position).

If you think about how young babies act when they're carried, they sit more chair-like when they're supporting their head and neck, and have a better pelvic tuck when they're snuggled in. This is all linked to this reflex. As they get older and they voluntarily go into more active or passive positions in-arms (and in slings/carriers), they tend to do the same.

When they're smaller, this practicing of neck control also triggers the upper spine to straighten more, by way of this reflex. When they're learning to hold the weight of their head there can be lots of bobbing backwards and forwards, triggering this reflex. Being carried upright actively contributes to spinal development. Having this reflex helps with both positioning and practicing straightening the spine in small doses.

Moro reflex

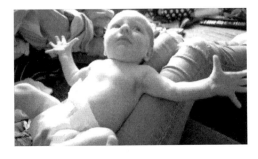

Extension (first reaction when triggered)

Flexion (second part of reaction)

The startle reflex is triggered by things like sudden movement, loss of balance, or sudden loud noise. It presents as an extension of the limbs first with a startled look, then flexion, sometimes accompanied by crying. In more extreme reactions there can also be a "frozen" reaction in between extension and flexion.

When this reflex is tested, it's generally elicited by pulling the baby up by their hands a way, then letting go. This triggers a strong reaction. In the pictures above, the reflex was triggered by the baby's own movements (feeling unstable) and didn't result in freezing or crying, just a startled look.

In carrying, the first part of the reflex would serve as a risk-of-fall warning, which triggers the person carrying to hold baby tighter/stop them falling. The second part of the reaction brings baby back into the physiological position and into secure contact with the person carrying.

As the reflex integrates it's replaced by the adult startle reflex, which generally exhibits as a "jump" reaction, shoulders shrugging, a gasp, tension of the arms and legs, and sometimes a jerk of one of the legs. This tends to be elicited from a sudden fright, and the reaction to falling is generally a righting reflex. As previously mentioned, it's not uncommon to see both the palmar and plantar grasp reflexes elicited by the Moro reaction, showing that this reflex is more complex than it seems at first glance.

Also interesting is how it's been shown that if a baby is grasping with both hands when this reflex is triggered, only the flexion and adduction part (the second half) is elicited.[6] This adds yet more weight to this being a carrying reflex, and I would go a step further in my suggestions. I've noticed that this reflex also exhibits only the second half in carrying, even if one or both hands are not clinging. I wonder if bodily contact of the arms and closed fists send a similar signal to holding on with hands?

Stepping/walking reflex (or "Clinging adjustment reflex")

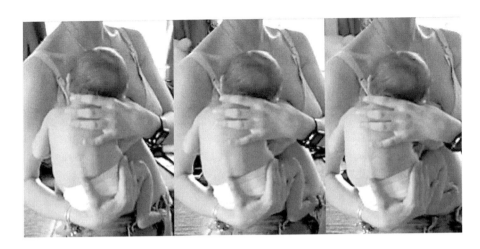

Foot brushes waistband, foot and knee draw up, full flexion & forward motion of the leg

This is one of my favourite carrying reflexes. OK, I know what you're thinking! "This doesn't look anything like the usual test for the stepping/walking reflex". I know - and there's a very good reason for this. It's a reflex that seems to have been completely misunderstood and named incorrectly.

The "stepping" reflex is usually discussed in a way that it re-emerges at a later date or that the reason it's not useful in the beginning is because walking requires balance and the ability to hold our bodies up. Why on earth would we have a walking reflex so many months before we're even able to hold ourselves upright? What purpose does it serve, especially developmentally? Well it serves a great purpose if you throw out the "stepping/walking" idea and test it out in a different way!

When tested in the usual way, babies are held upright and their feet are placed or brushed on a solid surface. The response elicited is a flexion of the leg - it's a massively exaggerated "step" because it's not a step. When tested like this there is a second part to the reflex – extension of the leg after a pause during flexion. I hypothesise that this happens because the leg has nothing to come into contact with so reflexively disengages.

When babies first cruise and walk, do they walk like that? No! Why would the "stepping" be so pronounced? Because it's not stepping, it's flexion and abduction of the legs, drawing them up close to their abdomen. The forward motion is to move the leg close to the person carrying's body.

In carrying, this is happening when the feet brush the body or clothing of the person carrying. It rights their positioning, getting them back to the even spread-squat position if their legs start to relax (slide down). The trigger is stroking or pressure on the foot, and it works in conjunction with Babinski's sign and the plantar grasp, which are activated depending on the way the reflex was triggered. The plantar reflexes work to either grab or stabilise with their foot as they grip back on with their legs. When this reflex is triggered, up to 24 muscles simultaneously activate![7]

Think about how each of the primitive reflexes integrates as the postural reaction related to said reflex takes over. What postural reaction comes as the "stepping" reflex integrates, if we view it as a walking reflex? Nothing! Standing unaided happens many months later and walking comes after that. Even crawling is months off. Yet if we look at the reflex from a carrying angle, the progression to a postural reflex is clear - the conscious righting of the leg positioning on the person carrying's body.

When this "stepping" reflex is elicited on a flat surface to attempt mimicking walking you can clearly see differences between walking when the true reflex emerges and similarities to its use in carrying. If you look up videos of the reflex in action, you'll see that the "step" is usually fairly quick when triggered, but that babies generally pause at the top, as if it should stop there. After a pause the leg will lower at a slower rate. When I watch these from a carrying-centric train of thought, what I see is the reflex to right their position and cling on, then the body realising there's nothing to come in contact with so disengages.

Foot placing reflex

This reflex produces a similar response as the "stepping" reflex, but is elicited by stroking the top side of the foot. It's usually tested by stroking the foot on the edge of a desk so the baby then places their foot on the table (hence the name "foot placing reflex").

Again, this is to do with reflexively adjusting their position in-arms and prevents them from dangling when sat on the body. The same quick pulling upwards of the knee happens as in the previous reflex.

Lower extremities/"Clinging reflex"

Xander, 4 weeks

The position babies' legs go into when they're on their backs or picked up - spread-squat - is a reflex that I haven't been able to find discussed anywhere. We know that it's a reflex action, as it's observed from birth when conscious and voluntary actions aren't present.

This reflex begins to integrate when babies start to be able to consciously disengage from being carried. This becomes a postural reflex, triggered by knowing that they are going to be carried (e.g. being lifted up), going into position, and disengaging (straightening the legs) at will when they want to get down, or don't want to come up. This is another reflex that would be great to have more research on, especially in relation to carrying!

It's obviously very useful as a primitive reflex action – it wouldn't be of much use if babies stayed straight-legged when we attempted to carry them would it? It would still be unhelpful if we had to manipulate them into a carrying position after bringing them to our bodies. Further still, when they are lacking voluntary control in adopting the carrying position, it would make carrying much harder work for the caregiver/s, in terms of practicality and energy expenditure.

It's interesting to note how these reflexes tend to work in harmony with each other, and how more than one reflex can be triggered at a time, making the combined response more powerful. Even the sucking reflex can trigger a stronger grabbing response – particularly useful for breastfeeding on the go! So these reflexes, working in harmony with each other, form the main carrying reflexes. They enable babies to be carried more easily in the early days, weeks and months when they are less stable and are gaining muscular strength.

As the primitive reflexes are integrated, conscious, voluntary movements take their place. So, for example, the palmar reflex develops into conscious grasping of objects. The "stepping" reflex to right the position in arms becomes a conscious and voluntary adjustment. Or if they don't want to stay up they will consciously leg-straighten! The plantar reflexes become voluntary balancing, gripping and stabilising movements. The Moro reflex (in terms of carrying) develops into an awareness of falling and the baby will consciously try to hang on (using, in part, that integrated palmar reflex!). The tonic labyrinthine reflex develops into the baby being able to keep their head balanced and look around without triggering whole-body extension.

As each reflex integrates, the body is stronger and more developed. The baby now becomes a voluntarily active participant in the carrying process - if we let them. Without the understanding of the learning process their bodies go through, it can be hard to know what to do to encourage them to hang on.

As all these handy reflexes disappear, and their bodily control increases, we tend to shift our carrying support to lower down their bodies, ending up using very passive holds.
Working with their new voluntary actions, you can help them build up clinging strength and stamina, keeping them active participants and making less work for yourself. This enables you to carry them for longer periods of time, and contributes greatly to their development. In case my wording is off, they don't suddenly lose muscle tone and need to rebuild it though – they just now have a choice as to whether they will happily engage or not, which can result in refusals based on their new-found independence (commonly seen in babywearing).

I always thought it was clever how as babies and children grew bigger and heavier they were able to get around more, in the sense that as they grew bigger they would be carried in the sling less. With in-arms carrying, you've got the added benefit of them being able to work harder and for longer with holding on too. This also makes a lot of sense - if they're heavy and need carrying, it'd work better for the person carrying if the child could do more of the work!

This is mandatory with my children, if they just want to come up (e.g. not if they're upset, hurt or tired) then they know they have to share the work or they can walk!

A note on deviations from the norm

Not all babies behave in a classic, textbook way. Even those who do most of the time still deviate from "normal" at times. Sometimes things can interfere with the reflexes, such as hyper- or hypotonia or gastric issues. Sometimes reflexes are missing completely, which is an indicator of an underlying issue/medical problem.

Disruption of reflexes may be a one-off, happen occasionally, or be a long-term thing. An example of a one-off or occasional disruption to a reflex is the back arching and that comes with "colic". Things like pain can override a reflex temporarily.

If the disruption is a long-term one then the reflex may become retained and the body/brain continues to "practice" the movement long after it should have integrated. This can have significant effects on children and adults throughout their life, and can be an indicator of health issues.

It's useful to read more about the reflexes and symptoms of retention, but if you're in any way concerned at all about your baby or child's development, please see your GP or other qualified medical professional for further advice/investigation.

Chapter 6

Progression to Postural Reflexes and Voluntary Actions

We know that the primitive reflexes integrate and are replaced by postural reflexes and voluntary actions. We also know that the age of integration is in relation to physical development and coincides with developmental milestones. For example, the palmar grasp fully integrates as the baby consciously holds onto things. When we look at the reflexes used in carrying, what milestones correlate with integration, and see what they are replaced by, it gets all the more interesting.

These replacement reflexes and actions are essential not just for active carrying, but for the journey from being carried exclusively (in the parent/carer's arms, sling/carrier, pram etc.) to being able to get around by themselves. They help with balance and keep us upright and aligned. It's a beautiful, complex, and intertwined progression that carrying clearly helps with.

In carrying

As we know, getting from primitive reflex to postural reflex or conscious, voluntary actions is not a "switch off, switch on" process, but a gradual and overlapping one. The postural reflexes can be involuntary, like the primitive ones, but can also be overridden by the brain through conscious choice. For example, as they develop, the instinct to bring the legs up when a baby/child is lifted can be overruled if they don't want to be carried. Overruling reflexes begins before a reflex integrates, a bit like how children and adults can teach themselves to overcome certain impulses.

Postural reflexes are grouped into righting reflexes and equilibrium reactions. The equilibrium reactions are to do with balance, and happen subconsciously, but their movement response is event specific and unique to each situation. Righting reflexes cause the head and body to move back into an upright and aligned position.

Most of the postural reflexes stem from the midbrain. Their appearance indicates maturation of the nervous system, as the primitive reflexes are controlled by the lower brain (reptilian/primitive brain). The midbrain makes up the upper part of the brain stem (with the primitive brain below), and – among other things - is responsible for sending messages to the upper (conscious) brain so that we can recognize and respond to reaction.

Although both of these parts of the brain are within the brain stem and the midbrain takes over control of many reflexes from the primitive brain, it's still possible for the brain to function otherwise normally even if one or more primitive reflexes don't integrate. The lack of integration will interfere with other development but not the brain as a whole.

Some postural reflexes and voluntary actions seen in carrying which follow on from primitive reflexes include:

Head and body righting reflexes

As the TLR integrates the head righting reflex enables instinctive postural adjustments. This reflex enables them to bring their head back up if it's not upright. This is again caused by the vestibular system, with the labyrinth in the ear signalling the disorientation to the body. Body righting reflexes allow them to adjust their position back to a stable one if they become unbalanced.

Grabbing

Voluntary grabbing with their hands is used for several things. Grabbing an arm or clothing can help stabilise them (postural response), or be used as an ongoing means of support. Grabbing may also be used as a way of being picked up. Isaac's favourite way to be picked up is by grabbing hold of my forefingers and swinging his legs up as I pull him up.

This grasping action is one that can be encouraged by the usual ways such as giving them objects to hold or holding their hand. To further develop their abilities, you can provide them with opportunities to hang/swing on things as they grow. Hanging is the starting point for eventually being able to pull your whole bodyweight up with your arms (think chin ups, pull ups). Being strong enough to do this enables you to pull yourself to safety when you can't use your feet or legs to help you climb up.

Hanging is also very useful for when babies and children are exploring, climbing up things. If they slip, having a good hanging ability can prevent injury. In carrying, it's helpful for holding on if you lose your grip or they decide to disengage.

Holding

You'll find that they use their arm and/or hand to balance themselves and keep them stable (postural). Hooking an arm around yours, or around your body, is a classic holding action. In a shoulder carry, the arms are responsible for much of their holding onto you, and the legs tend to be more passive; your shoulders essentially becoming a chair.

You can help develop this action by verbally or physically encouraging them to hold on when they come up if they don't instinctively place an arm or both arms in a stabilising fashion. It will soon become instinctive for them.

If they have a preferred position but it's not comfortable and/or practical for you, just attempt to work with them. Carrying requires teamwork, and it has to be right for you both to be enjoyable and comfortable. Communication is key, even when they are pre-verbal. It builds trust and understanding, and can strengthen your bond. If they are really adamant, you may need to compromise by either adapting positioning or using a certain hold for shorter periods of time.

Once you've both found what works well for you with their arm/s, you can play with how much work they are doing with it. You may find that they either increase their muscle activation, or decide to use other muscle groups to counter the reduction in support.

Climbing

They can also assist in getting onto you by using their legs to climb your body as you pick them up, and their hands and arms to pull up. This is a skill that can be encouraged by normal play, and practiced any time you carry them. Again, this is something I do regularly with Isaac, as he's still light enough to let him hang from my fingers and climb up. It's transferred well to playing for him, as he will happily climb up even a cargo net at the park.

Gripping

The inner thighs, calves and feet are all parts of the lower body used in being an active participant in carrying. Which part or parts they use will depend on the hold used and how much they are participating in the carrying process. If you provide more support for their lower body then they will grip/cling less. Providing support to the upper body requires them to hold on tighter with their lower body.

An extension of this is letting them slide down your body when they want to get down. You can initiate this by slowly removing support so that they have time to realise they need to hold on (and verbal cues help too), and providing a little support if needed. It can be quite fun for them!

Encouraging gripping with the lower body will help with things like control when sliding down a pole at the park, climbing trees, and holding onto static objects.

Disengaging

Another voluntary action is the disengagement cue in carrying. It can range from a simple straightening of the legs to indicate they want to be put down through to extended rigid legs and body accompanied by protesting and/or crying when they are fighting against being carried. It's a useful indicator of their want for exploration or it being a bad time for carrying (and babywearing).

Although there will always be times when disengagement may be harmful to them (e.g. while crossing a busy road), when it isn't it's helpful to respect their need to get down. As I've mentioned, we're born inherently active beings and it's only the impact of a sedentary society which slows us down and makes us reach for the easiest solutions. As they become more mobile, in-arms carrying becomes intermittent. There's always something interesting to explore…..until they want a cuddle again!

Disengaging is a milestone on the path to full independence. Remember how as they get bigger and heavier they become more mobile, therefore we don't need to carry them as often?

Disengaging is part of their way of communicating that need for independence.

The emergence of these reflexes and actions are entirely dependent on the baby's unique development, so focus should be on how they are progressing as opposed to expecting things to happen by a certain age. Working with the baby at their stage of development (so not doing extra work for them if not necessary) and encouraging them to engage more when they're happy and willing will help by providing the opportunities to practice the movements and progress naturally.

As with the primitive reflexes, the postural reflexes and voluntary actions work in harmony to create the carrying response. As these take over it becomes easier to work with them to create a reciprocal carrying process. With all these in place, and the baby now having good overall control of their body and balance, variations can be used both for targeting specific areas of the body for practice and giving areas a rest when tired. It becomes less necessary to adopt passive carrying positions the more the clinging behaviour has developed.

Looking out for and recognising the integration of primitive reflexes gives you valuable information to define your unique carrying experience. You will be able to work with them to develop each of the clinging behaviours further as and when their voluntary actions emerge, rather than trying to work with carrying as one action.

It may seem either enlightening or daunting when you realise how much goes into creating a seemingly simple behaviour. If it's daunting, try not to think of it as all these things that need to work perfectly to create a baby who actively participates in the carrying process. I know how it feels. When I'm learning something new in trampolining it inevitably requires several actions to be performed in a sequence to complete the move. It also requires those actions to happen within the space of a few seconds maximum. It's easy for me to see in my head how to do it perfectly, but transmitting that information to my body and getting it to do them in that timeframe inevitably doesn't go so well.

Thankfully with carrying, the person doing the most actions is the baby or child, and they are hardwired for learning and adapting. Also, the integration of reflexes happens at different stages so you're not suddenly confronted with a bunch of new behaviours to work with. In a normally developing baby, giving the right stimulation is all that's needed to help them progress. How much and how quickly they progress will of course be individual to them.

Remember, the capacity is there but all babies and children develop at different rates (some excelling in auditory skills while their motor skills develop more slowly, for example). Also, even if they are developing well, some will have a better natural capacity than others, just like every area of development. So don't worry if you don't end up with a superhuman clinging machine! Like I've mentioned previously, all 3 of my children who have had the benefit of my in-arms knowledge have different clinging capacities, regardless of the practice they've had. They're all different with regards to their general areas of expertise, and have shown me both how much is possible to achieve and also the limitations of the individual.

Chapter 7

Spread-squat and Postural Development

As babies develop, it's interesting to see how slight variations of the spread-squat position factor into every one of the postural milestones all the way through to walking! It's important for maintaining balance, and it's no coincidence that it appears at all these stages. As they move through the developmental stages the legs straighten out more, but a voluntary squat is still used once walking is complete. The squat and spread-squat are normal human behaviours designed to be used for life.

Sitting

As babies learn to sit unaided, they use their arms as a way of propping their upper body up. With the lower body, the hips are open, knees splayed, lower legs angled in, feet angled in, sometimes touching. This is very similar to the in-arms hip position, just at a different angle. The palmar grasp would need to have integrated before they can sit unaided, as they need to be able to use their hands to stabilise themselves as they progress from propped up by their hands to sitting upright without them.

Once they can sit unaided their position stays similar for quite a while, gradually straightening their legs out as their development progresses.

Isaac, 6 months

Crawling

During the stages of learning to crawl, the spread-squat position is seen in different variations. When they lay on their front, arms supporting the upper body, their legs lie slightly bent out to the sides. When they're on their hands and knees before being able to propel themselves forwards (think hands and knees rocking!) they tend to adopt a spread-squat position. If they try crawling "commando" style, they'll move their knees upwards and outwards, one at a time, to propel them forwards.

Xander, learning to crawl

When normal crawling commences, their knees come forwards and slightly outwards as they move, one at a time. Again, their legs and orientation of the movement ends up straighter as the skill develops.

Pulling up to standing

Pulling themselves up to standing begins the straightening out of the legs in full, in preparation for walking. It's from here that we begin to see less of an inclination to draw the knees up when lying down. Babies and toddlers won't have legs that appear fully straight until around 3 years of age.

This is all to do with keeping a wider stance to help them balance when walking and even though the bow-legged look disappears; their gait doesn't reach full maturation until around age 7.

This is just fascinating to me. You know I said I thought it was interesting the way we develop, getting stronger as we get heavier, meaning we can do more for ourselves as it becomes ever harder for our parent/carer to cart us around? Well, the gradual loss of the abducted knees in walking just seems to correlate so well with the increase in length of leg and the increased ability to cling onto more of the body at will.

Cruising

Again, the legs are still slightly bowed, and they will continue to be for quite a while after they've learned to walk. A wide stance stabilises their body, making it easier for them to learn to walk.

Climbing

As babies learn to climb, they use a combination of crawling and stepping actions. As they get older and stronger they become more dexterous at it. Active carrying teaches the clinging behaviour which can aid climbing (e.g. trees) by enabling the climber to hold on with their inner thighs, calves and feet. It also allows practice of climbing up the person holding them, using their hands, arms and feet.

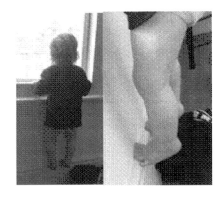

Isaac, 17 months

Logan, 5 & 6 years old

Standing

When they begin to stand unaided their usual stance is feet wider than hip-width apart, feet angled slightly outwards and a slight bend to the knee. They're progressing with the straightening out of the lower limbs, but still need a wide stance to keep their balance. They don't need to adopt a new way of holding their body – they just use the position they're already used to!

Squatting

Squatting unaided is very similar to the spread-squat in-arms position. Babies get to the floor from standing by lowering themselves into a squat. When they can stand unaided they learn to stand back up out of a squat without holding on to anything.

As they master walking, you will see them begin to adopt the partial (or what I call "active") squat, where the spine is straight, bum comes further away from the legs and the thighs are parallel to the floor. This is used to pick things up from in front of them, and requires more balance as their centre of gravity is shifted forwards. It's a quick squat - they don't tend to spend much time in it, unlike the full squat.

Isaac, 16 months

The full (or "passive") squat is the classic position babies and children go into for either resting or doing something close to the floor without sitting. Knees are either in line with, or slightly wider, than the hips, and the feet may be angled slightly outwards. The spine is straight or rounded a little, depending on what they're doing. Their bum is close to both the legs and floor and the thighs touch the calves. This squat is a very deep one.

Xander, 4 years

Walking

When babies first start walking, their gait is very different to adults. It's a straightened out version of the spread-squat, with knees bent out to the sides and lower legs angled slightly outwards. This creates a wider base for them which helps with balance.

The plantar reflexes (grasp and Babinski's sign) stay until the toddler has mastered walking and develops good balance. It wouldn't be of any use for them to disappear any earlier, as they help them to balance as they get used to moving around upright and their gait (walking pattern) changes from essentially losing balance on either side to taking purposeful steps forward.

Toileting

If you've ever seen a toddler scuttle off to do a sneaky poo, you'll probably have observed them squatting to relieve themselves. A deep squat is the normal, healthy way to eliminate, and is preserved around the world in countries which use floor-level toilets/toileting.

The spread-squat is also used in natural infant hygiene to hold a young baby from birth onwards to help them relieve themselves. It's a position which is very helpful for aiding the passage of poo, and is a handy tool to use for nappied babies who are having difficulty eliminating.

Once they can sit unaided, some people use potties or a toilet seat, or a combination of in-arms and toileting aids.

With the high toilets used in the UK we soon change to a seated position, and invariably use this for the rest of our lives.

As you can see, this position which begins in the womb and is integral to carrying is also important in a whole host of developmental stages. Using the spread-squat in carrying keeps the chain of development unbroken, and I wonder what the implications may be of skipping it.

Chapter 8

Biomechanics of In-arms Carrying

We've looked at how babies are designed to be carried and how their clinging behaviour develops as they mature. Now, let's explore the technical side to carrying - how it works in a load-bearing way, how it impacts our bodies and how the person carrying and the person being carried can work together in harmony to create an enjoyable experience for both.

Active vs. Passive Carrying

Throughout this book you've probably noticed that I've mentioned active and passive carrying. I've given brief descriptions of what this means, but I want to clearly define it now, as I tend to use the terms in a broad sense.

Passive carrying is where the baby/child has minimal or no participation. This may be when they're asleep, or if they're being carries in ways where the person carrying them supports most of the weight, and the person being carried engages less of their muscles/doesn't really have to consciously work at holding on or supporting their body. Passive carrying isn't *really* passive in the true sense of the word, as there's always some input unless they're asleep, but it's the easiest way to distinguish between the balance of participation from caregiver and baby/child. They tend to feel heavier as you're doing the majority of the work.

Active carrying is where the baby/child is a participant in being held. They actively do some of the work (usually a fair amount), as well as you. The person being carried is engaging lots of muscles, which vary depending where they're being supported on their body. They have to use various parts of the body to cling/hold on, and as a result they feel lighter in arms as they're sharing the workload with you. Active carrying enables caregivers to carry the baby/child for longer periods of time as it's less taxing for them.

In an ideal situation, baby/child would be an active participant until they became tired. Passive carrying would happen at this stage, also when they are asleep. Some holds that I describe as passive aren't technically so, it's just that I describe passive carrying as the person carrying doing most or all of the work. We're going to look at common positions babies and children are held in a bit later on, and see how each one can be active or passive based on how the person holding supports them. Different muscle groups are activated depending on how you support the baby/child, for both them and yourself. We'll take a look at these too.

If you've used a sling/carrier with your child/ren then you'll have likely noticed how they feel heavier when they're asleep in there. This shows that even in carrying aids babies/children still do some of the work! Although some cultures use carrying aids which encourage active carrying, the sorts of slings and carriers we tend to use here are - at best - similar to passive in-arms carries.

Sensory input

Carrying requires input from the sensory systems of both the baby/child and the person carrying them. This works best with skin-to-skin contact, as there are no barriers, but obviously isn't always practical or possible. Finding time for skin-to-skin carrying will help you both.

To know how to respond to the messages being given through touch, the somatosensory system responds to changes on or inside the body. A mechanoreceptor is a sensory receptor that responds to physical pressure. Mechanoreceptors send messages to the brain to enable us to respond accordingly and tactile feedback comes from proprioception. Proprioceptors in the skin, muscles, and joints enable conscious and non-conscious reactions to the stimuli.

Basically this means that our bodies rely on the sensory input from different areas to be able to respond to the way the baby/child is sitting on us. Messages such as them relaxing their grip from their legs tell us to either loosen our hold (to send a message back to them to cling on), adjust their legs or create a shelf with our body (don't do this!).

The vestibular system (the sensory system which is responsible for our sense of balance and spatial orientation) works to coordinate movement with balance. The vestibular system senses changes to equilibrium and communicates the need for micro- and macro-adjustments in how the baby is sitting or holding. It makes you counter a child's leaning movements, and makes them right their body if they slip.

Both caregiver and baby/child respond to touch in carrying and it tends to be the main way of communicating the need for positional changes. By avoiding bulky clothing you are able to make it easier for these messages to be sent and received.

Loads

When we carry, we're adding a load to our body. If that load can do some of the work to make them lighter, it has to be a bonus! A great thing about carrying in-arms is that babies and children tend to be fidgety. This means we tend to shift them around, holding them in different positions, which gives different muscles in our body a chance for both activation and rest. Even with passive carrying we're told by our own bodies to change position so distribute the load over different areas of our body so it's not left to one group of muscles to do all the work. Changing up positions and where on your body you're carrying provides you with a good range of muscle use and gives your baby or child a healthy range of movement and muscle activation.

That being said, it's not uncommon for them to develop a positional preference. It's happened with Isaac too, and I only have to look at my upper arms to see a marked difference in size between the left and right! When this happens it's even more important to pay close attention to how you're holding your body and listen to what it's telling you, as its doing multiple times the work it would usually do. It's much easier to end up out of alignment without the counter-actions of holding on the opposite side of your body (front/back, left/right).

It's always important to remember to be aware of our posture and alignment (more on that in the next chapter) so we don't turn our carrying into bracing the "load" against our body. This is incredibly important when it comes to some postural issues and/or bodily dysfunctions. By leaning our bodies in certain ways to brace, the flexor and extensor muscles of the trunk can be burdened in a way which induces back pain.

Creating excessive curves in the spine creates undue pressure which impacts the spinal discs, increasing the chance of injury. The vertebrae are meant to be stacked in a specific way so that the discs can then cushion them, absorbing shocks and movement. When we misalign our spine it isn't protected in the same way.

Also, things like pelvic organ prolapse (POP) can be exacerbated by bracing the weight of a baby or child on the body as the weight and position causes an unnatural downward intra abdominal pressure.

We need to be aware of how the weight of the baby/child can impact our bodies, especially negatively. Learning how carrying works and ways of protecting different parts of the body will make it more comfortable and enjoyable for you.

Caregiver's spine

We've looked at babies' spines and how important it is to protect them, but what about adults? It's incredibly important to protect our spines too, and they tend to be affected to a lesser or greater degree in carrying depending on how we're carrying and what our posture and alignment is like.

The best way to protect our spine include is to keep our bodies aligned. Avoiding sticking your hip out and not using your body to give you leverage (no rib or hip thrusting forwards or backwards) are simple ways to do this, and we'll explore postural and alignment corrections, and the difference between normal alignment and alignment in carrying, in the next chapter.

Now, let's look at how each part of the spine moves, and it's relevance to carrying.

The load-bearing parts of the spine are the five lumbar vertebrae (lower back) and the twelve thoracic vertebrae (upper back). The lumbar vertebrae support the upper back and head, and help with posture. They are the largest and strongest in the spinal column, and are the major load-bearing area of the human body. The twelve thoracic vertebrae carry and support weight of the rib cage. These also play an important part in posture.

To be able to take on the task of carrying extra weight without injuring ourselves we need to take care that our spine is load-bearing in the way it was designed to. This can look different to normal alignment due to how the muscles respond to loads (we need to protect these too) and the effect an extension to our body has on our centre of gravity.

Cervical spine

The cervical spine is your neck. It can move in all directions, flexing forward, extending backwards, rotating left and right, and bending to the sides.

This tends to be impacted with back carrying, when people compensate by bending their head forwards. Keeping your head upright will protect the cervical spine.

Thoracic spine

This is the upper back, parallel to your chest, where your ribs are attached. It can rotate but doesn't bend backwards and has very limited forward motion. Having minimal movement means that the organs within the ribcage are protected from being crushed. The thoracic spine is key to our stability and helps hold out body upright.

This part of the spine can end up being bent in a hunchback from poor posture. It's important to make sure you're not hunching over when carrying, and if you need to provide some resistance it's done with a straight back.

Lumbar spine

This is our lower back, from below the ribs down to our pelvis. It bends in all directions, but doesn't rotate.

Negative ways in which we may use the lumbar spine in carrying are to do things like sticking our hip out to the side, moving our pelvis forward and backward, and sticking our ribs out. Injuries are more likely here due to the flexibility.

Sacral spine

This is comprised of pelvic spine, sacrum and coccyx. These bones are fused together so have no movement at all.

Muscle groups

Lots of large muscle groups are used in carrying. It is a whole-body activity, and I'll talk more about this later. The caregiver uses various muscles in the arm/s based on how they're supporting the baby/child. The muscles in the trunk stabilise us as we carry the extra weight, and our leg muscles and glutes enable us to walk while holding them. The movement patterns used in carrying contribute to a strong, healthy body.

It's difficult to pinpoint the exact muscles used in carrying, as so many are used in varying degrees (and I've not studied to a high enough level to accurately pinpoint them all!). We can, however, identify certain groups and recognise how much input they may have during different holds or carrying motions.

The main muscle groups that will *always* be used in carrying when standing upright are:

- Psoas
- Quadriceps
- Hamstrings
- Calves
- Chest
- Back
- Abs
- Glutes

Other groups most used depending on the part of the carrying process or support provided are:

- Shoulders
- Biceps
- Triceps
- Forearms
- Hands

During the lifting phase of carrying, the muscles of your hands, biceps, triceps, the long and short flexors of the forearm and trapezius muscles are doing more work. When you're supporting with one or both arms, your biceps, triceps, forearms and shoulders tend to be at the forefront of muscle activation in the arms.

Arguably, the most important muscles of the body are the illiopsoas. These large muscles join the upper body to the lower body from the lower spine to the top of the femurs. It's also attached to your diaphragm, so is activated when breathing too. The psoas muscles are responsible for many things, such as supporting our pelvic and abdominal organs, our range of motion in the hips, pelvic alignment, moving our legs, stabilising the hips and so forth. They are the strongest of the hip flexors, and many of us end up doing damage to them by spending too much time sitting.

In carrying they are responsible for supporting your own body and the extra weight from the load. They provide the range of motion needed to partially squat to pick them up, aid in postural support and help move our bodies. These are also responsible for babies and children bringing their legs up and adopting a spread-squat position and supporting their bodies.

We'll take a look at ways in which we may harm this very important muscle group every day in Chapter 10.

Centre of gravity and line of gravity

Some ways in which carrying becomes harder for the person doing the carrying are to do with the body's centre of gravity (or centre of mass) and line of gravity. Our centre of gravity (CoG) is usually just above our belly button. Our line of gravity (LoG) runs like an invisible line from the top of our head to the bottom of our feet.

When we're holding things, having them close to our *centre* of gravity keeps us more stable and less likely to fall. Holding them close to our *line* of gravity keeps them feeling a more comfortable weight. The further away from our LoG, the heavier they feel. So if it's on top of your head it's right on the line of gravity, and if in your arms but close to your body it's a little away from it. If you're holding something out in front of you, it's even further away from your LoG.

So, keeping them close to both our centre of gravity and line of gravity helps with carrying. Of course, we hold them in different positions on our body, including on our shoulders. It's interesting to see that most carries (especially instinctive ones) tend to have the baby/child in a position which lines up well with our CoG, and keeps them close to our LoG. In a shoulder carry however, even though they're quite far from our CoG, they're much closer to our LoG, which makes carrying them easier.

Protecting joints, tendons and ligaments

In carrying there is flexion or extension of different joints depending on what the body is doing. Being mindful of which ones you're using will help protect them. For example, not bearing the weight of a heavy baby or child on your hand will protect the wrist joint.

Tendons connect muscle to bone and ligaments connect bones together at joints. Their purpose is for both connecting and enabling movement. Sometimes our tendons and ligaments can be put under pressure from carrying, so it's important to be aware of how you're using different parts of the body. Our shoulders and wrists tend to be at risk, as it's not always at the forefront of your mind to pay attention to what your arm or arms are doing.

Shoulders tend to be vulnerable because it's easy to slip into a relaxed hold as opposed to an active one. When this happens the weight of the baby/child pulls on these ligaments rather than the muscles doing the work. This can result in shoulder pain and also encourages more passive carrying. You can easily correct this habit by sliding the humeral head (ball of the upper arm bone) back up into the socket of the shoulder.

Wrist tendons and ligaments are put at risk when you bear their weight in this area or create a pulling motion during hand-clasping. A common injury from carrying is De Quervain tenosynovitis, which is an inflammation of the tendons on the inside of the wrist by the thumb. It's possible to hold your hands or wrists when carrying without putting them at risk but it requires correct distribution of their weight further away, and holding hands/wrists in a way which doesn't create oppositional forces.

Asymmetrical carrying (carrying on one hip) can cause a compressive force on the hip joint beyond what is needed to bear the weight. It's important to make sure you're not sticking your hip out to brace their weight. Doing this creates contraction of the lateral flexors on the opposite hip, and extension on the side carrying, which also causes the intertransverse ligament on the carrying side to be strained.

In simple terms, this means you may end up with lower back and/or hip pain because you're compressing one side and extending the other, while putting an unnatural amount of force in place. By using a smaller amount of movement and being aware of where that movement is coming from you will protect your body better. A push-pull movement from your lumbar spine (lower back) will create the classic stuck out hip and dropped ribcage on the opposite side. The impact on your lower back is not good.

The hip is used to great amounts of load-bearing. Your legs are supported by them and they're responsible for moving your legs when you walk. It's no wonder the hip is an instinctive and natural place for us to carry our babies and children. It seems to be normal to create a small amount of extension of the hip in carrying, usually when we're standing still. That we have this range of motion, but it has the potential to cause harm if used for extended periods of time suggests that it's something to be used in small doses.

If you think about how we walk, our hips move side to side to compensate the shifting of weight from one side to another. There will always be a certain degree of "hip sway" in carrying, even if you try to keep perfectly aligned. The hip joints are made to be able to bear this "misalignment" without injury.

Thinking about adding an extra load to the hip, you may wonder if this would have a negative impact. I don't know for sure, but my take on it is this. As we grow and get heavier, we're adding bigger loads to our joints, and our bodies adapt to this. With gestational parents, they get used to additional weight as the pregnancy progresses and the weight then shifts up to their chest once baby is born and carried in-arms. We also carry different loads in every day life, and a baby wanting to sit on your hip generally tends not to be an excessive load (unless you're not used to it).

Gestational parents' hips are generally shaped to create a "ledge" of sorts, which provides an area to cling onto. It seems that they are biologically designed for hip carrying, especially when you add in the way babies fit the hip in a jigsaw puzzle piece sort of way. It does raise questions as to what the "normal" is for non-gestational parents when it comes to carrying. It's very noticeable to me that cis-gender men do not default to hip carrying, and that the ways in which many carry suggest that – biologically at least – carrying babies is designed to be a primary role of the gestational-parent.

This isn't to say that *only* they should carry. I'm acknowledging that the most "nutritious" way of carrying seems to work better with gestational parents and those born with biologically female bodies. Our bodies are designed in a way that we can withstand many less-than-optimal influences and still thrive. In my mind, I see the differences in body make-up as ways of meeting evolutionary needs. Some things take priority over others, and the shape of bodies surely has some relation to this.

To protect both your hip and spine, remember to create the movement from the lumbar spine in the direction you need rather than creating a bigger, bodily movement to move. It will mean you won't overextend your hip or spine.

Another protective measure is remembering to move your whole body when reaching for something or turning. Using your feet to turn rather than rotating the spine will protect your body from positional strain.

Forward planning can also be helpful. How long are you likely to be carrying for? What will you be doing while carrying? You can lessen the risk of hurting yourself by working out any obvious risk factors. For example, if you're going to be going on a long walk and you're not used to carrying; do you have a baby carrier or someone going with you who can share the carrying? It's important to not overdo it, and build your strength and endurance gradually.

Children carrying siblings

It's worth adding a note about older children carrying younger siblings. To protect their bodies, if they're carrying for a length of time it's important to remember that it's not recommended that children and teenagers carry more that 10-15% of their bodyweight.[1]

This is easier to measure if using a sling or passive holds, but active carrying eases the burden. It's more important to be aware of if they carry regularly. It's also worth recognising the ways in which their spines are impacted when carrying heavy loads, and applying that knowledge to improve the care of our own spine.

Chapter 9

Posture and Alignment

We've taken a look at what makes babies so well built to be carried. We know that babies are "clinging young", and (in most cases) are born with the necessary reflexes to enable the carrying process. We've also looked at the biomechanics of carrying, and how the caregiver's body works and responds to the carrying process. We've touched on how important it is to factor in posture and alignment when it comes to carrying, and now I'd like to expand on this.

Our posture and alignment can make baby carrying easier or harder on our bodies. Many of us have to work consciously to keep in alignment and adding carrying to the equation can distract us from making sure our bodies are protected. Our bodies generally form with good posture and alignment as we grow, as they are designed to work this way. Over time, our habits tend to erode the biologically normal body and repeated lengths of time spent in bad postures can eventually change our alignment, which can cause wear and tear to our spine.[1] In the next chapter we'll explore ways in which we harm our bodies and ways that we can begin reversing any damage we've sustained.

Many of us throw our bodies out of alignment in an attempt to make carrying easier, which tends to result in actually making the process *harder*. In some cases, depending on the severity, length of time and repeated use, postural changes may be found (as seen in studies regarding posture, load-bearing and the spine[2]) and can sometimes result in injuries to our body.

We tend to misalign our bodies the most when we don't encourage natural clinging behaviour, but can still unconsciously do it when we have. The instinct towards the "easy option" is interesting as its instant gratification behaviour. Even if we know that misaligning our body will result in paying for it later, many people will still subconsciously slip into these behaviours.

You may recognise this in the way a school child will be told to sit up straight yet ends up slipping back into a slouched position. It's not usually conscious – it's the result of repeated behaviours which then impact on the body. You may also notice this when driving, that you sit in a good position when you first get in, but as you drive you eventually notice you've slumped in some way.

Sedentary lifestyles have made resting the default and have altered the physiologically normal body of many people. I think that this is why our subconscious tends to gravitate towards short-term "easy" options in carrying – because we're used to reaching for them in lots of other areas of our lives.

We'll explore this more in chapter 10, but for now let's take a look at what correct and incorrect posture and alignment look like and how they can impact on our bodies.

Regular alignment

When we're standing, good alignment looks like this:

Note where the line of gravity falls, where the arms are, where the thumb and fingers are pointing, and the general shape of the spine from the neck downwards.

Now, here are a couple of examples of misalignment:

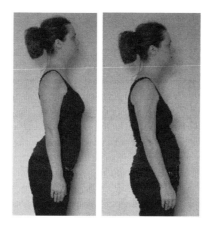

Hips tilting forwards/thrust backwards and hips tilting backwards/thrust forward (with slumped shoulders)

Again, make note of your observations, and how they differ from the previous photos.

Alignment is important for more than just good posture – it affects many areas of our health. It's important for spinal health, for sure, but also our health and movement in general. Correct alignment helps your body to move efficiently and reduces the risk of injury. All the major systems of the body work better when we're aligned. Misaligned bodies mean our internal organs are affected, by pressure from the ribs, spine and/or pelvis.

To be aligned you need a neutral spine. Each part of your body needs to be "stacked" correctly on top of each other – head, shoulders, ribs, pelvis, and feet.

Let's take a look at 3 things which (individually or collectively) contribute to poor posture, and how these things may be exacerbated during carrying.

Posterior pelvic tilt

This is where you bring your pelvis forward by tilting it backwards. Your lumbar spine is flattened. The rectus abdominus (abs) are shortened causing them to weaken. It also results in tightened glutes and hamstrings and reduced range of motion in the hip flexors, amongst other things.

Depending on the severity and how long it's left untreated, some of the possible outcomes include degeneration of joints, chronic lower back pain, disc herniation and hip pain.

Anterior pelvic tilt

This is the opposite of the previous example – here you're making an exaggerated arch in your lower back by tipping your pelvis forward.

If left untreated your spine can also change further up to compensate, resulting in stooped shoulders and your head sticking forward. Like with posterior tilt, back pain, disc herniation and degeneration of joints are all possible results of this postural condition. Also, your abdominal muscles lengthen, hip flexors lengthen and hip extensors shorten.

Lateral pelvic tilt

This is where the one hip is tilted and higher than the other. It's linked to people with different leg lengths, and hereditary conditions. It's also brought on by environmental factors which can be a cause of scoliosis (sideways curving spine). One cause of obvious importance when in comes to carrying is carrying heavy loads on one side of the body. It can range from mild to severe.

When it comes to carrying, proper alignment before we start carrying is important. For many of us with existing postural issues, we don't have the time to reverse these ongoing issues before we carry (for example, if our baby/child is already here and needs carrying now!). Even if this is the case, we can still do as much as possible to correct our posture and alignment when we're carrying.

For example, we can "reset" our posture before picking them up (examples of this later on in the chapter), make sure we're lifting them up correctly, and re-adjusting our posture as we notice it slipping.

As you will probably appreciate, if we have existing issues we're likely to slip back into these postures when carrying, and the added weight of our baby/child can contribute to exacerbating both the poor posture/alignment as well as adding more stress to the spine and joints.

This is why I'm vigilant with banging on about posture and alignment. With in-arms carrying, we have no clue as to the damage we may be doing to our bodies. Even with babywearing in the UK, we may be further on in our understanding of it, but there's still a strongly held view by the majority that "any babywearing is good". Whilst that's true in the sense of our babies being held close, it's the polar opposite for our own bodies and the potential impact on our future health.

Those who know me well will have heard me say on more than one occasion that it will be interesting to see the impact on our own bodies in the years to come, especially if there are some scientific studies conducted (side note, there's at least one study proving the possibility of postural changes when using slings[3]). I'm obviously just as interested in what we may find about the impact of different ways of carrying in-arms!

Alignment in carrying

It's been shown that most ways of carrying (as in, where we carry something on our body) create low levels of spinal loading – our bodies are designed to carry things.[4]

When I was working to improve my in-arms carrying alignment to encourage clinging behaviour, I was noticing a great improvement in comfort. In pictures though, I realised that although my body felt in correct alignment, I had been instinctively doing various little postural adjustments which made it look like I was misaligned. If I was comfortable, not experiencing any pain or other issues, and my osteopath wasn't finding any alignment issues, could it be that alignment in carrying is different to "normal" alignment?

Intrigued, I did some research on in-arms carrying in cultures which don't have sedentary lifestyles to see what their carrying in-arms looked like, on the premise that I'd likely see similarities. I found the same positions used for carrying, and similar micro-adjustments in posture. I also investigated the range of motion of our spine and hips, and how we use our arms in carrying, as well as studies on other load-bearing activities and the human spine.

The results of my studies seemed to show that alignment in carrying *is* slightly different to normal alignment. When we're carrying a load we're both adding extra mass and weight to our body and how it needs to be stacked is going to vary based on how we carry our baby or child. This has led me to believe that it is normal to make some natural postural adjustments, and I think I know why we do.

Remember the centre of gravity? Without something strapping our baby/child to us, it becomes more important to work with our centre of gravity. If we change position, we shift our centre of gravity. This helps keep us stable, and different adjustments are made for different types of carrying. The key is to work with the body's natural movements for each carry rather than going too far and hurting ourselves.

With hip carrying, our CoG has shifted closer to the side on which we're carrying our baby/child. To counteract this shift in CoG, a slight adjustment to the side we're carrying on stabilises our body. Just like if you stand on one foot, your CoG moves over to that side, and you shift your weight onto that leg, and may lean more to that side to balance.

With hip carrying, if you stand upright and aligned, then ease your spine slightly to the side you're carrying, you should feel it as an easy and natural movement. Your spine stays straight and moves slightly to the side.

Now try sticking your hip to the side in the usual hip-sticking-out motion. Not so nice is it? Ribs drop down towards your hip and the lower spine both curves and twists. Think about adding the weight of a baby or child onto this and you can imagine how this isn't so great for your spine. Also, you're actively shifting your CoG further as you're effectively leaning away from them by creating that deeper ledge.

If we stayed aligned as we would when not carrying, we'd be less stable and they would feel heavier as they're further away from our line of gravity. Also, our centre of gravity has moved, but we've made no bodily adjustments for this.

Being more aware of the location of your CoG and being able to work with it will help you to use your whole body less to counteract the additional weight of the load you're carrying. It may even make moving more comfortable for you.

The composite centre of gravity when carrying is the combined CoG of you and the person you're carrying. This shifts from you towards them, in whichever direction they are from it. It doesn't necessarily move a huge amount though. Remember it's to do with the weight distribution from your whole body. For example, an older baby who weighs 20lbs when you weigh 140lbs is just 1/7th of your total body weight.

So if they're on your shoulders it will move slightly upwards. If they're on your hip, it'll move slightly towards the hip they're on and also forwards towards their body. Having an understanding of this can help you greatly with posture, alignment and how you balance your body.

"Shifting" your centre of gravity?

It's been put forth that it's possible to move your CoG without physically moving your body in the direction needed to stabilise yourself.[5] Whilst this sounds amazing and the testimonials of people who've tried this technique may draw you in, this is physically impossible. The centre of gravity is based in physics, and is the centre based on the weight distribution and shape of the object.

Also, the idea with this technique is to "lift" your CoG *upwards*, which would make you less stable (remember, a lower CoG provides more stability).

What you *can* do is consciously shift your balance, and move more easily, based on your mindfulness of where your CoG is and how you need to balance it out. The mental "shifting of CoG" in the reference provided really can work, but it's to do with body awareness rather than moving something with your mind.

The technique linked to is really handy for keeping aligned and stable in positions where you may usually throw yourself out of alignment to adjust to your new CoG!

As our CoG is not a static point (it also shifts as we move) we have to make many reflexive micro-adjustments. This tends to come easily once we've made our adaptations to compensate for the original shift. Think about how much of a conscious effort you initially need to make to balance on one foot, compared to the smaller adjustments to stay balanced once you're steady. It's like this with carrying too.

These postural adjustments tend to be used more when we're standing still. I feel this is the case because active carrying is a type of *movement*. Yes, babies and children can (and do) still cling when we stand still, but active carrying seems to be more conducive to the dynamic carrying process. Even though we're the ones walking, the movements we make move their bodies and hips and they actively counteract our movement. It's like a beautiful dance!

I know I've noticed that I tend to do a slight shift when still, as Isaac goes more passive when we stop. I don't know whether this sort of behaviour is linked to our tendency towards passive carrying, in that we're signalling in some way to them to be less inclined to hold on, or if the clinging instinct is less without our motion. It's definitely an area worthy of further exploration.

I've also noticed that I don't do it as often with Logan, who has the most incredible clinging abilities. I'm not sure if it's to do with longer legs meaning better leverage for him, or how hard he clings, or a combination of both. Whatever it is, I do shift my balance to the side I'm carrying for stability, but make less spinal/hip adjustments.

Another postural adjustment is how we hold our shoulders when using and arm or arms to support the baby/child. To support them, you need your arm to be in a certain position. When supporting higher up their body you're able to keep your shoulder closer to its normal position. When you're supporting them lower down your shoulder may need lowering. You can feel the difference between lowering your shoulder and pulling on your ligaments by doing these two tests.

First, hold your shoulders in the neutral position and put one hand on the opposite shoulder. Now, shrug that shoulder up and down. The shoulder comes up and down and the trapezius muscle expands and contracts. It should be a comfortable motion. Next, move your hand to the edge of your shoulder, with your middle finger on your shoulder bone and make a pulling motion with your shoulder. You should feel your shoulder bone pull down and towards your ring finger. You'll likely also feel pain or discomfort in your trapezius and bicep. A good video to watch to correct from ligament carrying to muscular carrying is "Baby holding without shoulder straining" on the Nutritious Movement YouTube channel.[6]

I must stress though, that you don't necessarily need to make sure your shoulders are in the normal "standing in alignment" position – they should be aligned for the weight-bearing activity you're doing. Our shoulders have a natural range of motion like the rest of our body. This may mean your shoulder may look out of alignment to the other, or may look like both are "rounded" to the untrained eye.

The difference between misalignment and alignment here is where the weight is being borne, and how it actually feels for you, the person carrying. Knowing the difference between what ligament-bearing and muscle-bearing feels like is important. Getting to know how your body works in terms of range of motion of your joints and what's comfortable for you is also very important. We have figures on the "normal range of motion" for different joints, but we're not carbon copies of each other. The normal range for you may be different than for others, and there may be underlying causes for this which may need attention, as well as the possibility of you needing to take extra precautions.

Another concern is if you're focusing on non-carrying alignment you may risk hurting yourself or making carrying more difficult in other areas. For example, when I was first into the alignment stuff, I would regularly fatigue my arms as I was engaging the wrong muscles, trying to replicate a non-carrying posture. I'd also question why clinging seemed harder for my baby, but I thought it was because he'd gotten used to my misalignment. In fact, it was a combination of that and not understanding that alignment in carrying is different.

As much as you nurture your baby or child's clinging ability, there's always going to be a point where they just can't hold on any longer, or the angle they're on you is just not conducive to them balancing correctly. Finding the balance between providing the correct body positioning for yourself and not being afraid to let them do the work will make your carrying journey more comfortable.

With back carrying and shoulder carrying, there's a tendency to pivot slightly forwards to adjust to our new CoG. The child is creating an extension behind us, and if you hunch over, you're creating excess pressure on your spine. Of course, adjusting your body to your new CoG is needed and simply staying completely straight would make you less balanced. Aligned adjustment is certainly possible by being aware of how you adjust your neck and/or body to compensate - keeping the spine straight and hinging from the hips keeps it protected and the weight bearing in the correct places.

Try it yourself: stand upright and aligned and try pivoting forwards from your hips. It should feel comfortable and easy to do. Now try leaning forward in a more hunched position. This is what we tend to do in shoulder carrying to make it easier to balance them. Our spine is rounded and the weight impacts on our upper back and the compression can continue on further down the spine depending on the weight. Added to this is the fact that we then need to keep our heads up most of the time to see where we're going so that's creating an additional curve in our neck.

One way we may misalign our bodies when back carrying is excessively sticking our bum out to create a ledge for them to sit on. This creates pressure on the lumbar spine and pelvic spine, and can alter our upper body's posture too. Providing additional support or encouraging more active clinging eliminates the need to do this. It can almost seem instinctive to stick your bum out, as the limited range of motion from your arms combined with the inability to see them right there in front of you means you're attempting to compensate.

While some compensation for the carrying load may be needed, and we know that our lumbar spine has a good range of motion, it's important to make sure we're compensating in the right place rather than creating a ledge to bear their weight on. Again, an aligned spine along with a hinging motion works well here.

For front carrying, there's a tendency to thrust the hips forward, to brace the baby/child's weight. This again creates undue pressure on our lower spine, plus creates a downward force to our abdominal and pelvic organs.

With a burping hold, we tend to thrust our ribs forward, then our hips and shoulders back to stabilise. As with all carries, the key is to keep in alignment and either encourage the baby or child to participate more with the carry or provide additional support so you don't feel the need to brace. Adapting your alignment to how you're carrying when need be is important, as is good posture. It's important that we look after our bodies to avoid strains or injury.

It's even more important when carrying during pregnancy, when people are more susceptible to over-extension of joints with the increased laxity that comes at this time. It's also a period of time where lower back and pelvic pain is more of a risk factor. There's more on carrying and pregnancy in the chapter "Special Considerations".

It can be frustrating when you're trying to correct your posture, as so many things affect it over long periods of time, every single day. Especially when your body is so used to being is a bad posture, and it feels like coming into alignment takes effort and feels strange. It can feel like a never-ending battle, but it is so worth it. Any positive changes are better than none, and especially when carrying, babywearing or lifting. Adding extra loads to a body with poor posture and/or alignment just exacerbates it.

Posture and breathing

Did you know that poor posture can affect how much oxygen we can breathe in, and breathing can also affect posture?
Classic sitting posture on a couch is with the pelvis tucked forwards and the ribs bearing down. This inhibits our lung capacity, meaning even if we tried to take a full breath, we wouldn't be able to fill our lungs to their actual capacity. For example, rounded shoulders restrict how much your diaphragm can rise by, the expansion of your ribcage and your lung capacity. Aligned shoulders open up your chest. Tilting our pelvis back and dropping our ribs also impact on breathing.

Now think about holding a baby/child in a bracing action against your body at the front. That extra load may also impact on your lung capacity, making carrying that much harder, as well as you already needing to take in more oxygen to compensate for the additional weight.

If you focus on your breathing, it can help you to correct your posture as the more you're aware of your lung capacity or lack of it, the more your body should try to help you optimise it.

So when we carry, there are a few checks we can make to see if our posture and alignment is off. If anything needs correcting we can use some quick postural adjustments to get back in alignment.

Head/neck

A properly aligned head and neck means the cervical spine isn't being overloaded. If your head tends to lean forwards at all, you're creating additional load for your spine. You know how a baby/child feels heavier the further away from our body they are when we're carrying them? Well the same thing is happening with our head. The further away from fully aligned, the heavier our head feels on our body.

We tend to bend our head/neck forward a lot due to mobile phone use, tablet use, looking down as we walk, writing, working or playing with our laptop/computer too low, having the television at a lower than eyelevel height etc. It can feel like our head is slightly tilted backwards when our head is aligned if we're used to a forward head posture, as what feels like central is actually still too low. It takes time to get used to the normal angle.

Physiotherapist Mark Wong lists some exercises on his website to both check for and help correct forward head posture.[7] Check out the citations section at the back of the book for the link.

If you need to make any adjustments for carrying, make sure you use the pivoting motion of the first and second vertebrae in your neck rather than a bending forward and down motion.

Shoulders

The most common alignment issue with shoulders is slumping them forwards. To check your alignment, note where your arms and hands are in relation to your thigh. If they're forward of the middle of your thigh and your thumbs are pointing towards each other, then you're slumping forwards. Your arms should hang round about in the middle of the side of your thigh, and your thumbs should be facing forwards.

To correct your shoulders, perform an exaggerated roll from front to back. Start by lifting your shoulders as high as you can, then slowly roll them back, then slide them downwards. You should feel like your upper back muscles are slightly pinched in. Your chest will be more open and sit higher.

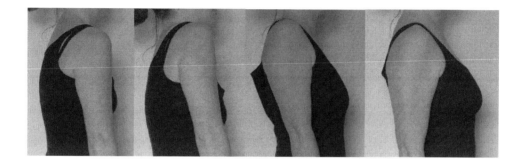

In carrying, you're looking to have an open chest, whether your shoulder/s are in normal alignment or have adjusted downwards depending on how and where you're supporting. Again, make sure the weight isn't pulling on your ligaments!

Ribs

Rib thrusting is a backward lean of the upper body. Katy Bowman has a great blog post to check for rib thrusting and explains the difference between this and swayback, which it can be confused for.[8] There's also an exercise to help reverse it - again, check out the citations section for the link!

We tend to thrust our ribs in carrying when we carry higher up on our front, as a way of using our body to bear their weight. As you can imagine, our body isn't designed to bear weight this way and it impacts on our spine as well as our ribs.

There's no need to adjust to carrying by leaning backwards. If you feel the need to do this, your baby/child needs more support from you (e.g. use your other arm to support their upper body instead of letting them lean onto your chest).

Pelvic tilt

Having an anterior (front) or posterior (back) tilting pelvis creates either an excess curve in the lower spine (anterior tilt) or flattens it (posterior tilt). It can be a bit confusing (or is it just me?), as the tilt of the pelvis is the opposite direction of what it looks like!

Anterior tilting is used to create a ledge with your bottom in carrying and posterior tilting creates a place to rest your baby/child on your abdomen. Use your arms to support them better, or encourage them to cling on more instead of thrusting. When they're on your back you can compensate with an aligned spine rather than sticking your bum out.

> One of the best and quickest ways to do a whole-body adjustment is to imagine you have rope attached to the top of your head and it's pulling upwards. This will make you correct every part of your body in unison.

So, alignment in carrying follows many of the principles of non-load-bearing alignment, but requires awareness of where the CoG is and how to safely adapt your body to it. Starting with correct normal body alignment and making adjustments from that point will lessen the risk of you hurting yourself.

Also, alignment may vary based on whether you're standing still or moving. It's definitely possible to lessen the need for postural adjustments if you change how you're supporting them, but this isn't always possible. Knowing how to adjust in a safer way will protect your body.

> All of the suggestions listed here are designed to give you ideas for at-home temporary measures to keep your posture and alignment in check. This does not replace professional advice and treatment, and I highly recommend seeing a professional if you either suspect or notice you have any issues.

Alignment in babies

It's also important that we keep aware of our babies' alignment. Babies benefit from good alignment and paying attention to how their body is stacked will help you to identify any potential issues.

We're looking to make sure their head, neck and spine are all in alignment most of the time. Sometimes they will have their head turned to one side, of course, and this is fine. Making sure they spend as close to equal amounts of time with their head turned to the left and right will help prevent uneven muscle lengthening and shortening. Turned to the left, the muscles in the right side of the neck lengthen and the muscles in the left side shorten, and vice versa when turned to the right.

In the early weeks and months you may notice a side preference or leaning issue with your baby. For example, some babies will prefer turning their neck in one direction, others may have a hip/leg slightly higher than the other and some may lean to one side.

It's always a good idea to see a professional about this sort of positional preference, especially when unaligned, to check for any problems. Sometimes there's an underlying issue (e.g. muscular tension) and other times it seems to be just a phase.

Here is an example:

Izzy's preferred position is left leg raised and left shoulder dropped, causing a sideward curvature of the spine

As you can see, Izzy is not in alignment but is very much chilled out here. Positional preferences like this can stem from their position in the womb. Sometimes it can be to do with their position during birth or the after effects of instrumental delivery. For many babies with alignment issues with no underlying issue, it rectifies within the first few months post-partum with no additional help. Izzy's positional preference corrected within 2 months post-birth.

Isaac had a left-leaning preference when he was born. He saw an osteopath regularly from newborn to a few months old, and he had no alignment issues. He was also assessed by a different osteopath when we went to a private clinic for tongue tie assessment, and she also found no alignment issues. This was a case of positional preference, so I supported him in this position when he was adamant about being in it, and encouraged him into alignment when he was cooperative.

So what do you do if your baby sits on you in misalignment yet there's no underlying issue to be found? This can be tricky as a parent, as if you know the importance of alignment it can seem counter-intuitive to carry if they sit misaligned.

It can be argued that carrying them when they're not in alignment wins over not carrying because of positional issues. The argument for this comes from the huge benefits of carrying in other areas of their development, as well as the flexibility you have when carrying in-arms to encourage positional adjustment as and when they're reciprocal.

As always, check with your care provider for anything you need to be aware of and/or work on with them for this unexplained misalignment, but if there is no advice I suggest listening to your baby (please still do this anyway alongside any medical advice!), and working with them to find the best way of carrying for you both. Encouraging positional changes when they're receptive and supporting them well when they're "wonky" (to take pressure off muscles, ligaments and the spine) may help with easing back into alignment. Being the people who spend the most time with them, we have a unique insight into their behaviours, quirks, and times of day when they're most receptive to therapeutic measures etc.

Babywearing may help with holding babies in a certain position, but it seems to be something which doesn't always work as a corrective measure, especially if how they hold their body deviates more than a little from what's normal. The lack of fluidity of support and movement means they're held in a static position until you change their position. In arms, you're able to respond to positional needs as they arise and it's generally much less restrictive in terms of tension on the body.

It's certainly an option for attempting to "train" the baby's body into optimal positioning, but don't be surprised if they go "wonky" despite your best efforts. To pin them in the preferred position means excessive tightening which may impact on other areas of the body (joints, spine, neck etc.). With enough wiggle room to not feel restricted, there's invariably room to get comfy in that preferred position.

Chapter 10

Helping or Hindering our Bodies?

Trained to rest

Arguably, many of us have spent our lives being taught in subtle – and not-so-subtle - ways to rest our bodies as much as possible. If you went to school, or did school-type work at home, you will probably have spent many thousands of hours sat in passive positions, likely also unaligned, neck bent forwards etc.

The increase in the use of technology for both work and play encourages much of the same. Laptops, tablets and mobile phones tend to be used in ways which encourage our heads to be in a bent forward position. This can leave us with forward head posture, which can contribute to slumped shoulders and neck pain.

Also, comfy sofas and armchairs encourage slumped posture when sitting. The definitive solution to this is to be a "furniture free" household, but that's not something the majority would want to do, so I'm not going to push the idea, although I will say it's something that makes a lot of sense.

So how do we counteract these limiting effects? How do we prevent these issues for our own children? What has the biggest impact with the least investment may be your biggest question. We're usually our biggest critics and knowing that we need to do better often places great burden on us knowing that there are other, more pressing, things which need our attention first. Thankfully there are many ways we can either preserve or improve ways of looking after our bodies or those of the people we're looking after.

I try to have an approach that is far from "all or nothing". From my own personal circumstances, having ways of improving our quality of life with small increments rather than needing to commit time and/or energy that I know I don't have spare, means that change actually happens. Okay it may be over a longer period of time but I know that I'm more likely to stick with it as it has less of an impact on our lives overall and the changes sneak up on us in wonderful ways.

I have 4 children. I home-educate and am self-employed, with a husband working full-time. Life is fast-paced here, even when we're actively trying to slow it down. I find it incredibly difficult to do better. I hope that you'll find that at least some of these suggestions may fit into your own lifestyle and that improving yours and your family's health doesn't seem like some mammoth task.

We're going to go back to the beginning and discover the many ways our bodies may end up developing to make it harder and less comfortable to carry our children, based on lifestyle choices made by ourselves and our parents/caregivers. The following is a timeline of common lifestyle choices and other situations we may have no choice over, with suggestions on how to lessen or reverse the impact on our bodies.

Infancy

From the moment we're born we can have postural and/or alignment issues. Our position in the womb, how we were born, the position we arrived in, any instruments used, and how we were handled during and/or after the birth can all have effects that may not be picked up on for weeks, months, years or even ever! Some things we have control over and others we don't. Being aware of what can cause problems gives you a heads up to keep an eye out, make informed decisions where possible and seek treatment if need be.

Osteopaths and chiropractors are some of the professionals who work with babies, children and adults to assess if things are out of alignment and treat any issues (there are ones who are trained to treat babies). As a side note, I feel strongly that osteopathy should be available on the NHS for all newborn babies. Even feeding can be affected by tension in the jaw.

Now, let's assume baby is all fine and is developing normally. Arguably, one of the first things we actively do that can negatively impact a baby's posture and alignment is putting them in a car seat. Obviously these are essential for keeping babies and children safe during car travel so are very much needed! The problems lie in the both type of seat used[1] and how long babies are kept in them for. Sometimes long trips are unavoidable, but there are plenty of times where we may be able to make a choice whether to keep them in the seat or not, such as when we get home.

Choosing a pram which doesn't rely on you using a car seat as the pram seat when they're little is another one. I remember getting a travel system with my first, not having any clue about the dangers of them being in car seats for long periods of time. It's difficult even when we do know, if we need a car seat and the only affordable option is one that comes with a buggy, but baby is too little to go in it without the seat. We obviously make decisions about what equipment gets the most investment, based on both our income and priorities.

Obviously I need to mention again about the "containerization" of our babies in prams, car seats, bumbos, slings/carriers, door bouncers and baby walkers etc. One thing we can do is keep an eye on how much time they spend in each of the "containers" they use to get an idea of how much time overall is spent in them, and how much time they have for freedom of movement.[2]

Slings/carriers need a special mention here, as – although they do restrict movement – they provide physical contact with the caregiver. The many benefits of babywearing may outweigh the downsides in your specific situation, making extended wearing something that's both needed and ideal for your family.

Working out where time can be cut down will mean you're free to choose what things you feel are absolutely necessary for your family, what things can be cut down (or removed completely) or what could be replaced by a more ideal "container" for the situation you're in (e.g. swapping car seat for pram, or pram for sling/carrier).

Once they're sitting, we don't necessarily start sitting them in a chair. Many parents are content with their baby sitting on the floor playing, which provides unrestricted sitting and freedom of movement.

It tends to be around this time that door bouncers or jumperoos are introduced. The marketing strategies of these devices is to "aid in the development of strong, healthy bodies" or a variation of this line. In fact, they are holding them in an unnatural position for their stage of development, are restricting the normal range of movement for babies at this stage and implying that you need a contraption for them to develop well.

These devices have their place, of course, for example to entertain a baby while the caregiver does something, but they are not essential – or needed in any way – for healthy development.

Something to keep an eye on, as they develop and grow, is how they sit. Do they sit on their sitting bones or tailbone? My middle two sit fine most of the time, but stick them in their car seat and they will *shift their bum to sit on their tailbone* – every single time! I have no idea why, but constantly having to remind them to go back to sitting normally is wearisome.

Are their legs stretched in front of them, crossed, or behind them? Being aware of any "W" sitting is important, as this is detrimental to their health. "W" sitting is where they're sat on their bum with their legs bent and rotated behind them at their knees. This increases the internal rotation of the hips beyond what is the physically normal range, and reduces the external rotation, making normal sitting more uncomfortable and changing the normal range of movement of the body.

The legs also become bent outwards over time, causing "pigeon toes" and the tibia (lower leg bone) to be angled away from the midline. This affects gait, balance, can cause issues with the knees and places undue strain on the joints.

Once they're standing unaided, they begin to squat down to do things lower down. Have you ever noticed how perfect and beautiful that squat is? Remember the pictures from chapter 7?

Squatting is wonderful for doing things closer to the floor, and can be a natural resting position too. The overuse of chairs and other seating begins the journey to losing the squat if it's not a regular movement you actively choose to do in life. Encouraging this natural position as they grow up will contribute to a healthy range of motion within their body.

We can do this by encouraging activities at squat-level and providing squatting toileting opportunities (e.g. low-level potties allowing them to eliminate in a supported squat, using a squatty potty stool to place your feet on, to installing a low-level or ground-level toilet if funds and inclination are there!).

Childhood

Shoes

Did you realise babies usually wear "shoes" from birth? In the form of socks, babygros or actual shoes designed for newborns. Of course, there are times of year when they need extra protection and warmth from the environment they're living in, but we are most certainly driven towards putting shoes on our young – in one way or another – as early as possible. Babygros tend to be the least offensive, if they're at least one size too big. Not allowing restriction of the foot is a bonus when covering their feet. There's some tactile disruption still, but when warmth is the priority, this, or a baby sleeping bag (or similar) really works.

Children need to be barefoot as much as possible for normal development, but obviously there are times when shoes are needed, and we need to make sure their feet are protected at these times. The issue is recognising the times when they actually need footwear and when they don't. For example, the insistence of shoe companies of the need for "crawling" and "cruiser" shoes is downright ridiculous. All they encourage is the early shoe-ing of our babies, with no proven (or theoretical) benefits!

As they progress to walking, the purchase of their first pair of shoes is something many parents do immediately, if they haven't already purchased those "cruising" shoes. This is another thing we do that can actively hinder normal development.

The thing to remember is how the shoes they wear impact on their walking, running and general posture. Any shoes which aren't designed with optimal posture in mind can negatively impact on your baby or child's body. This can also be a pinpoint for further postural issues depending on the type of shoes they wear.

At the bare minimum, new walkers being shod with anything with a "practical" sole will be missing out on time exploring their environment with at least some variation of physical contact with their feet. The "practical" sole tends to be quite structured, and the marketing is focused on providing "proper support" and encouraging "good foot health". In fact, it's conditioning biologically normal feet to become averse to nature and to need the "safety net" of added cushioning and/or support.

Think about it. If we haven't succumbed to the "baby shoe"

advertising then the most our babies have worn on their feet are socks. Why should they need shoes to "support" them as they learn to walk? It's advertised as a natural progression, but why would we have been designed to need a man-made product to enable us to do what we're designed to do as humans?

Feet not only need to feel the ground to respond to the terrain and stimulus, but our toes are there to grip, and help us balance. This is most noticeable when babies are walking for the first time (remember the platar grasp and Babinski's sign?) and it's no wonder babies and young children find it harder to balance and walk as smoothly when they're wearing shoes, with the hindrance of the full range of motion and body response.

"Cruiser" shoes can actually have great benefit though, if used at a later age than advertised. They tend to have very flexible soles, which make navigating the outdoors that much easier for babies who are walking. My own children (numbers 2-4) have used Inch Blue soft leather shoes in their early walking months outside. These are shoes designed for indoor use only, but work really well in the warmer and dry months outside.

"Proper" use of shoes is in the eye of the beholder. Where are you planning to use them? Will you be keeping an eye on the terrain or will they be running free? Will they actually be doing any walking at all? What protective measures do you truly need to employ? Questions like these will guide you to the answers you need.

For the first time, with my fourth baby, I invested in Stonz boots for the winter months, wanting to protect him from the cold weather, but in reality he wore them maybe 3 times. Yes, they were perfect for when he needed them (in terms of providing extra insulation) but they restricted his range of movement because – although very floppy and flexible – he was too short and too new to walking to be able to navigate them well. I'm looking forward to him being able to use them more comfortably this winter though.

Something to mention here as well is that things like these are fantastic for babywearing, to counter the riding up of trousers or to protect feet and legs from the weather in general. Insulated bootees are available far and wide for all budgets, so it's not just these I recommend, just the idea!

As they grow bigger you'll likely find a lack of lovely thin-soled, flexible shoe options. However, there are types of shoes called barefoot shoes which are designed to be minimal and better for the feet. These shoes ideally have a "zero drop" (flat soles), minimal thickness and flexibility in all directions. These types of shoes are the healthiest for both children and adults when shoes are needed as they are designed to keep us as close to barefoot as possible.

Unfortunately these types of shoes tend to cost more money, but are in line price-wise with some of the "trusted" and "best" shoe shops (e.g. Clarks shoe shop here in England). This can be frustrating though, if you have a tight budget. None of us wants to compromise our children's health, and feeling like we have no choice in the matter can be difficult.

Although there are specific "barefoot brands", it doesn't have to be something accessible only to those with more money. I've purchased several new pairs of shoes on eBay and Facebook selling groups at a discount, usually from parents who've bought in advance and their child had a growth spurt. You can also find excellent second hand shoes in these places, as well as taking advantage of sales from retailers such as Happy Little Soles[3] (UK retailer).

While there have been things said about not buying second hand pairs of shoes as they mould to the original wearer's feet, I feel that it's an individual's decision, and it's worth weighing up whether they're worse than structured shoes. Depending on the type of shoe, they may remould fairly well to the new wearer's foot.

I'm personally not too picky - my youngest two boys have worn their elder brother's old shoes from the first pair. They're worn so little at that age, and their feet grow so quickly, that it really isn't an issue to me. They're what are sold as shoes for "crawlers", so the thinnest of thin leather (or mock leather) soles; thicker than socks but more protective in the outside world.

As they grow, I need to invest in new shoes. Shoes are a big priority in my purchasing as they have a much bigger impact on my children's health than clothes do. Even before I was aware of the true implications of shoes on children's health, and I was a broke mum of one, I always made sure I scrimped and saved for a "decent" pair of shoes for my daughter. They were the priority of all clothing, as she would spend much of her waking life in them and I knew that a good pair of shoes would positively impact her health. Of course I was being fed the importance of a "good quality" pair of structured shoes, which actually weren't good for her health!

As my awareness grew, she would receive only barefoot shoes from me. Now, as a teenager, she has her own opinions about what she wants to wear on her feet, which can be frustrating. We tend to meet somewhere in the middle, with me scouring the internet for barefoot or close-to-barefoot options that fit with her wants, which is a bit easier now that she's in adult-sized shoes!

With my boys I feel I have more influence on their shoes. For a start, "boys" shoes are so focused on both comfort and practicality (y'know, because boys can have it all and be comfortable while they're at it) so barefoot variations aren't so dissimilar from their thicker soled and positive drop counterparts. It's easier to find options they like. I'm going to leave one last comment here about shoes, before I get distracted and go on a rant about the blatant sexism in the shoe industry!

By encouraging plenty of time barefoot and being mindful of the shoes we buy for our children, we can encourage their normal development and help them avoid health issues further down the line.

Preserving the squat

Years of wearing shoes that shorten tendons and muscles, as well as becoming less active and flexible, means many of us lose the ability to do a true, flat-footed squat. It's a case of "use it or lose it".

Active squatting not only helps our bodies with elimination, provides a different (healthy) way of sitting, and gives us a great range of movement; it can also assist in giving birth. Being able to untuck the pelvis creates more space for the baby to move down – or should I say, *not* untucking the pelvis creates *less* room. An untucked pelvis provides the *normal* amount of room. It also makes it easier for us to pick up our children (and other things) in a way which protects our bodies, and makes getting down on their level easier and more comfortable too.

If you have a walking baby or young child, watch them as they play. Notice them squat actively or passively depending on what they're doing. To preserve the squat, children need to keep active and do activities which encourage a range of movement and positions.

Teenage years

Most teenagers are living lives full of schoolwork plus multiple hours of homework each week. The stress of exams gets more intense the older they get, and those who go into higher education are doing this into their 20's.

By the time they're finished, most school children will have spent at least 13 years in full-time education, usually 30+ hours per week in school, roughly 39 weeks of the year, plus numerous hours of homework.

Carrying around of heavy backpacks and bags – especially wearing them 1-shouldered – impacts their body too. As I noted earlier on, it's also not advisable for them to carry more than 10-15% of their bodyweight. [4]

This is also a time where children tend to gain more independence and make more decisions for themselves. It may be a time where you find yourself having to make compromises when encouraging their good health. For example, my daughter doesn't like the "look" of barefoot shoes anymore, so I spend hours trawling the web trying to find ones that look more like conventional shoes. Usually she still comes up with something she doesn't like about them (logo etc.), so sometimes I compromise by finding better versions of regular brands, like for her trainers I just bought her!

A lot of things will hopefully just be ingrained and regular for them by now, if they've grown up with attention paid to movement, alignment and posture, so if they make decisions you would rather they didn't, hopefully the impact will be less. If this stuff is all new to your family and bad habits have become ingrained, there's going to be more work needed.

If you've got a teenager who is interested in all this, that's fantastic and they'll hopefully be miles ahead by the time they're an adult!

Adulthood

Once we reach adulthood we usually start our working life. Depending on what job we have this can mean continuing the sit-down work environment or being more active.

Driving can be a big contributor to poor posture, as it

encourages a slumped posture. I try to use this time to focus on how I'm sitting, and attempt to keep as aligned as possible. It's interesting how quickly a body used to driving slumped into the seat gradually moves back towards the position it's used to! Our spare time may involve exercising and being active in other ways, but many of us will find ourselves sat down, watching television, using our computers or browsing on our phones.

Sitting in general is something to keep a close eye on. It's been shown that even if you have a healthy, active lifestyle you are still affected by the amount of sitting you do.[5] Doing more physical activity doesn't cancel out your sedentary behaviours. The NHS has some ideas on how to reduce sitting time for all ages.[6]

As well as the metabolic health risks and higher chances of disease associated with sedentary behaviours, remember that prolonged periods of sitting also shorten some muscles and lengthen others, both weakening them and restricting our range of movement.

An easy starting point to improve our sitting posture is to locate our "sitting bones" (ischeal tuberosities) and make sure we're bearing our weight on them instead of our lower spine. They're knobbly and can be found by sitting on a firm surface and rocking your pelvis backwards and forwards. Once you've identified where they are, play around with your posture until your pelvis is aligned, your back straight and head and neck in alignment. This is where you need to be sitting, rather than tucking your pelvis and creating pressure on the base of your spine by sitting on your tailbone.

You may want to consider using a standing desk at work and/or at home if possible, and if not, try to have movement breaks often. Sitting shortens and tightens that amazing psoas muscle so it's very important to find ways to (ideally) minimize the time we spend sitting.

A quick mention again about shoes here as many of us spend a good chunk of our days shod. Heel height (even in "male" oriented shoe design) can negatively impact on our health through the changes made to our posture. Positive changes to our posture most certainly can benefit from better shoe choices, but both need working on. Many people find they need to gradually adjust to minimalist shoes if they've been used to structured ones most or all of their lives.

Heels shorten the calf muscle and increase Achilles tendon stiffness.[7] The higher the heel, the shorter position the tendons and muscles are held in. Heels also change our regular posture over time.[8]

As well as the type of shoes you wear, how they fit is very important too. If they're ill-fitting (too tight, incorrect size etc.) this can also lead to a whole host of problems. Good foot health is important for whole-body health. Both of these are conducive to comfy carrying.

Movement

Most of us need more movement in our lives. Have you ever watched a baby or small child when left to play without distraction? They're constantly moving, bending, stretching, changing positions. It's in their very nature to not stay still for long periods of time. It's only as they get older that this happens, and in actual fact it is actually enforced in most schools. Children are required to sit still and listen or do their work. Order is needed and that means minimising movement. Upping our daily dose of movement is good for our bodies and essential for normal development in children.[9]

We use the idea of "exercise" to reassure ourselves we're "active" but it's actually really abnormal when you think about it! Many of us are sedentary much of the time, and fit in maybe up to an hour, one or a few times a week, of time for exercising. While "exercise" is generally good, our focus should surely be on regular daily movement?

Movement plays a big part in keeping ourselves fit and healthy. Cardiovascular issues, constipation, mood disorders, low bone density and sleep issues can all be caused by lack of movement.

We've outsourced so much of our movement, it can be shocking to realise how much! It's probably partly why so many forms of exercise feel like a chore – our bodies are just not used to many and varied complex movements so are less primed for specific exercise methods.

Adding more movement into our days can be simple if we don't get overwhelmed by how sedentary we may actually be. We can start with very small things, such as getting up to stretch our legs every X minutes, walking the short trip to the shop/post office/park/school etc. instead of driving or using public transport, walking and talking, and getting up to make yourself a cup of tea instead of getting your child to do it. OK, maybe I'm not ready to give that one up!

Birth to 4-6 weeks

So, if we look at English post-birth traditions we see that there wasn't much carrying being done in the first 4-6 weeks after giving birth. This period of time was called "confinement" and has been practiced throughout history until as recently as the early 20th century. Confinement started in the final weeks of pregnancy, when they would be expected to stay in bed (the belief that this would help prevent premature birth) and lasted until 4-6 weeks postpartum, ending with a visit to church to be "cleansed" and to offer thanks to God for a complete recovery.

Babies were kept (as much as possible) in bed with their mothers. Mothers were given time to recover from the pregnancy and birth, and babies were able to slowly adjust to their surroundings. The confinement period was gradually lifted, in terms of what the new parent would be allowed to do. As time went one, they would be able to move to different rooms, but it was important that the baby be kept indoors during this time.

After confinement, life's triggered by positional movement, occasional upright lifting (infant hygiene, family member enabling sleep etc.), breastfeeding positioning and horizontal movement around the bed. Babies would be more upright and would get used to the continual muscular adjustments that come from being carried in-arms and supported by a sling/carrier (if available).

In this day and age it's not uncommon for the gestational parent to be up and about, doing a food shop or picking up children from school as early as the same day they gave birth! There's much pressure, both from society and the demands of family life, to get back to "normal" as soon as possible. It almost feels like it's a punishment for the continued campaign for equal rights, that pregnancy and birth is not respected.

So, many of us end up out and about very soon after birth, even if it was traumatic and/or required surgery. Our babies are exposed to much more than they used to be in the early weeks! Unless we've had both the time and inclination to honour our bodies' need for recovery in the weeks following birth, we're risking prolonging the period of time needed to heal and potentially exacerbating existing issues, which may impact on carrying.

New parents

As new parents we're then exposed to another bunch of situations where many of us aren't looking after our bodies. Breast– and bottle-feeding tend to be performed in hunched over positions, putting strain on our necks. Lugging around of car seats tends to have us misaligned, and possibly straining our shoulder too.

The way many pushchairs and prams are designed mean lots of people end up hunch over with handlebars too low. Other problems include standing too far away from the pram when pushing, ending up angled forward when pushing, which can contribute to lower back pain, and bearing weight on the wrists by bending them.

Living in individual houses rather than in a community tends to leave new parents isolated and sometimes to the point of exhaustion. More often than not, we're left with too much on our plate, even with modern conveniences.

Although lots of people will find their period returns before their baby/ies turn 1 even if they breastfeed, breastfeeding causes amenorrhea in many breastfeeding parents, which helps with natural spacing of subsequent children. Shorter spacing of children can leave our bodies facing extra stress by falling pregnant again before we've fully recovered from the previous pregnancy and birth – which takes a lot longer than a few weeks.[10]

Again, how we then carry our babies and children impacts on our bodies too, and by this point we may have already done a lot of damage throughout our lives.

Taking whatever steps we can to encourage recovery, recognising when we've done too much, and paying attention to what feels right and what doesn't will likely help make carrying more comfortable in the weeks post-birth.

As you can see, we end up exposed to so many negative behaviours throughout our lives that it's no wonder so many of us have postural and/or alignment issues, and niggling aches and pains.

The "Wall-E" effect

The Disney and Pixar film "Wall-E" presented a disturbing future for humans. One of the focuses of the animated film is about how humans effectively destroyed Earth with their harmful practices (throwaway culture, wrecking the environment etc.) and had to evacuate the planet. 700 years on, they are still living aboard a spaceship which has a cruise ship feel to it. The humans live in hovering chairs which give them a constant feed of TV, audio and visual stimulation. They drink all of their meals through a straw and are all so overweight that they can barely move.

Of course this is an extreme example, but it really doesn't seem impossible the way we're going. In this digital age we spend much more time sitting staring at a screen and are moving less and less. We're destroying our planet daily, and the powers-that-be are driven by the "advancement" of humans, often at the cost of our health in the most basic sense.

Yes, there are benefits to technological advances. The problem is there are so many disadvantages too, and there's not enough balance. Even when we're aware of all this it can be very difficult to make changes due to the fact that we're hindering our health at every turn.

The more we rely on aids in our lives, the less we move or activate muscles. Don't think I'm getting preachy and holier-than-thou on you - I'm a classic example of not moving enough and repeatedly doing things I *know* I shouldn't be doing. Know better, do better doesn't happen nearly enough as it should. We make priorities in our lives based on our individual circumstances, needs and health.

I need and want to do more, but I know that this will have to come at a later date if I want to carry on improving without burning myself out and giving up completely. Instead of thinking "it's all too much!" and resigning myself to the fact I can't do enough now, I make sure I do what I can right now. As a parent,

I prioritise trying to keep up the healthy movement habits with my children so they don't have this work to do when they're older. I benefit from these decisions; things like walking as a family instead of driving where feasible (which is still a struggle with a movement-averse 4 year old!), and I'm kept aware of my own body by way of prioritising theirs.

Things I do for myself specifically are choosing to walk instead of drive every time I can, take movement breaks when I'm working, I go barefoot whenever possible, and only wear barefoot shoes when I need or want to wear shoes. I realign my body as often as possible throughout the day too. It's a start.

Chapter 11

Physiological Carrying Positions

Now we're going to take a look at the most common in-arms carrying positions, how they may impact our body, any special considerations to bear in mind and what aligned and misaligned carrying looks like for each position.

This is a chapter to keep coming back to, to check how you're holding your baby/child and to note any recurring postural or alignment issues.

One thing I need to make note of is how I'm accustomed to carrying as a biologically female person. I do not have the lived experience of a biologically male person. It's important to recognise this, as I may feel I have insights into carrying from a biologically male point of view but I cannot give a true insight into the ins and outs of how this may work on a practical level as my body is built differently. If you're biologically male and find yourself drawn to how carrying works, I encourage you to record your own findings and explore your own insights.

Indeed, if you're biologically female and have an interest in this area, I also encourage you, too, to explore this developmental process further. Having multiple points of view, lived experiences and ideas will help further our understanding.

The following is a guide based on my personal experiences, observations of others and understandings and I hope it will be a good starting point for your own journey.

Aligned from the beginning

What I can do to get aligned and switch between active and passive front carrying is this. First up, I need to align my body before I pick my baby/child up. If I pick them up misaligned then I'm increasing my risk of injury. Here's how best (and how not) to pick up your baby or child when they're standing:

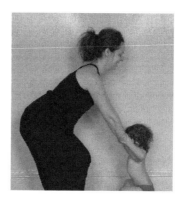

Aligned

Here my back, neck and head are aligned, my knees are bent, my hips are lowered back and I'm hinging my body forward at my hips. This was taken as I was lifting so I had squatted down further when first reaching him. As I lift him I reverse the hinging motion until I'm standing straight again.

Here I have straight legs and a curved spine. My head, neck and spine aren't in alignment. How I'm lifting means I'm creating excess pressure on my muscles, spine and knee joints.

Once I have them up in my arms, I need to maintain that good posture. By bearing their weight with my arms for a moment, I can check on what my body is doing and make adjustments if need be. Once I know I'm in alignment, I can then focus on their position on me. Encouraging a nice spread-squat position, with adequate support, will get them comfy and lays the foundation for alternating between passive and active carrying. I can now alternate the support I'm providing based on their capabilities and energy levels.

To encourage clinging behaviour, only support them at their upper or lower back, or fully support their legs at the thighs. This enables them to use their lower or upper body to provide reciprocal holding. You can still adjust the amount of support to turn this into passive carrying when they show signs of fatigue.

Now, just like anything in life, you're going to find yourself slipping into bad habits with little or no warning. You can either be hyper vigilant about this or take it as it comes. If your body isn't used to being aligned when carrying it *will* slip into misalignment to make it "easier" for you.

Whichever route you take, as soon as you realise what is happening, do the postural and support corrections. The more you do this, the easier it becomes to carry aligned. I promise. It may feel like it's so much hard work in the early days, weeks and maybe even months (depending on your postural issues), it really does get easier.

I've had very bad postural issues for many, many years, and it's taken a good 6 months of hyper-vigilance to get to a point where the work I'm doing seems small, and the issues much less. It kind of creeps up on you - you can half-arse it for years (like I did before!) and make some progress, or you can make some steadfast commitments in certain areas of life to make meaningful change.

Believe me stuff like this is incredibly hard for me. My priorities are my children's and my health, both of which command the vast majority of my time. The only way I started getting ahead was to work it into what I was already doing then once I nailed it, change up my "normal" to make more progress.

For example, in carrying it started as a matter of paying attention to how I was holding, and making adjustments as I went along. Once the new habits were ingrained I could work on how my baby or child was holding on, whilst keeping an eye on how this change impacted my posture and/or alignment.

In everyday life, thing like driving, sitting to write and walking in general gradually received upgrades. Making easy, incremental changes is definitely the way forwards. Not having huge expectations of a body so used to a sedentary lifestyle will save you so much time. It can be so tempting to push yourself, thinking "well I know I have the mental resilience to push myself harder!", but you *must* give your body time to adjust, build up gradually and gain strength and endurance. This process *cannot* be rushed – I can't stress this enough.

No matter how tempting, please don't fall into the trap of trying to do too much at once. The only things that will happen are big risks of:

- Injuring yourself

- Putting yourself out of action for a period of time, potentially impacting family life

- Getting disheartened by a perceived lack of progress and may feel less inclined to work on building up your carrying capacity

- Carrying on trying to do too much to try to prove to yourself or others that you can do it

This applies to all the carries going forwards too. You *must* give yourself adequate recovery time. This may mean a day or two of very little in-arms carrying. You can always use a sling or carrying aid on days your muscles need some rest.

Let's now take a look at different ways of carrying in-arms.

Front carrying

Carrying at the front of our body is done in different ways. Some ways we hold our babies and children at the front of our bodies are centrally, off-centre, facing forwards, in a cradle hold or even like a log!

When we carry on the front it can be easy to fall into misalignment traps. If you're used to passive carrying you may notice that you thrust either your ribs or hips, depending on the height you carry at. Babies tend to sit at a wider angle on our front and back than on our hip, and the front (and back) of our body isn't as conducive to clinging behaviour as the hip is. If you think about it, our front/back is flatter than our sides. Our sides offer a better ergonomic clinging place.

Babies and (especially) children *can* cling on the front and back – it just means approaching it differently and recognising there's a different set of rules and considerations. If you want a baby or child to cling to your front, they need to be able to hook their legs around your hips. Even if they can do this, they need encouragement to do so, as it's not as easy a task as clinging to a hip.

They may not be able to participate in active clinging for as long as they can on the hip, and they also may not be as receptive to clinging either. Their leg length may also come into play, as active clinging on the front and (especially) the back tends to work better when the baby/child's knees fit at least to each hip, enabling them to "hook" onto the hips, and sometimes even bring the lower legs and ankles past them and hold on with those too. Some will cling on just fine before then too – it seems to be a combination of the person carrying's body type as well as their clinging inclination and ability.

Some babies will be more inclined to use their upper body more than their lower body. These babies and children respond better to support lower down. Those who prefer to cling with their lower body more will prefer support higher up. Those who like both will be easier to work with alternating the support positions.

No matter their preference, if there are no issues then it's worth encouraging them working on the parts of their body which they prefer clinging with least. This will help them to gradually build up more strength here without putting lots of pressure on them. It's important that carrying is fun and/or comforting. A negative association isn't going to encourage clinging behaviour, and may do long-term damage to the carrying relationship.

I've noticed an interesting theme with biologically male parents of older (good trunk control) babies. For many, the trend is to carry off-centre on the front with the baby's legs in a bit of a scissor-like position.

I first really started noticing it with my husband, and thinking he held our children strangely, but when I looked to society in general I noticed it everywhere! I'm not sure why it's a "thing" but I do wonder if the toxic gender stereotypes make it more prevalent because of hip carrying being a stereotypical "mother" hold. I mean, even if you type "man holding baby on hip" into a search engine, you'll get a bunch of images of this front carry (and a whole load of pictures of women hip carrying!).

Another interesting search is "18th century man holding baby" (or 19th or 20th etc.) versus the same search but the word "woman" replacing "man". It kind of highlights the absence of men in the hands-on role of child-rearing (although the absence of pictures may well be to do with the hierarchy of importance at the time). If we speculate that men were indeed very much hands-off, maybe this would explain the difference in carrying technique?

Needless to say this is still a hold we see used by gestational parents too; it just seems to be more of a classic "dad" hold.

Cradle hold

This hold tends to be the "classic" newborn position, the one many people think of when they think about newborn babies. It's splashed over many forms of media and tends to be a person's first introduction to baby holding.

While the hold has its use, many babies prefer being upright. If your baby loves the cradle hold, that's great. Many babies are also fed in this position too, so it's an important one to look at to make sure we're protecting both baby and caregiver's bodies.

In the in-arms cradle hold it's relatively easy to support the baby's body and ensure their airways are unobstructed. The crook of our elbow provides neck support as well as having the range of motion to ensure their chin is off their chest. The forearm provides support for the rest of their body and can hold them in close.

This position is hard to replicate in slings and carriers, and is generally not advised due to the nature of the support provided, which encourages chin-to-chest, which restricts their airways. We tend to suggest an adaptation of this – reclined seated sideways – which is more upright but mimics the cradle hold better, without compromising their airways.
In-arms, the outer leg tends to hook up and over the lower leg.

Aligned

By supporting their body with both arms we're distributing the weight on both sides of out body. Weight-bearing with our forearms and just using our hands to rest on their body will help avoid wrist issues.

Misalignment with this hold comes in different forms. There tends to be forward leaning at the neck, keeping an eye on the baby, much like when we're feeding them. Doing this and moving our head back up can end up being a repeated process of misalignment, as it's not often we look up and down and consciously align our head and neck. One-sided preference in holding can also encourage the shortening of one side of the neck muscles and the lengthening of the other side when bending the neck regularly.

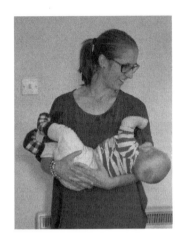

Misaligned

We can take steps to protect our neck by checking our head and neck are in alignment first, then using a pivoting motion rather than bending our neck forward and down.

Next, we may be bearing the baby's weight on our shoulder ligaments rather than our muscles. This tends to happen more when they're heavier, but extended carrying of a baby of any age whose weight in-arms we're not used to will cause us to tire eventually and increases the chance we'll slip into behaviours that seem to "help" us carry but actually aren't good for our body.

Another thing to be aware of is whether we're shifting to adapt to our changed centre of gravity.

Chest-to-chest

The chest-to chest hold is what we look to replicate in slings a lot of the time. Getting familiar with how babies behave in this hold, and essentially putting a sling around their natural position – as opposed to putting them into it – helps with respecting a newborn/young baby's physiological position.

This position enables a young baby to hear your heartbeat, which is especially good if you're the gestational parent as it's a familiar sound. With non-gestational parents it can still be a wonderfully comforting sound. This is also an ideal position for skin-to-skin contact.

Babies also seem to "slot" onto the chest quite beautifully for those with even small breasts. The shape of the breasts is conducive to that curved spine and knees up position. They lay against the chest at that sloped angle, and their knees tend to rest just under the breasts.

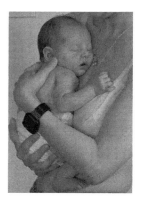

Isn't it wonderful, all the little biological things which we associate with certain uses but actually have their place in carrying too? The closer you look, the more complex (yet simple) the carrying process is!

Here are some examples of aligned chest-to-chest front-carrying:

Passive – aligned

In the first picture I'm supporting Isaac's legs with my arms and have my right hand gently resting near my left elbow. It's important to note that the weight-bearing is borne by my arms and *not* my hand or wrist. There are ways of holding onto your arm with your hand, or even clasping your hands, when carrying without risking injury. The key to this is making sure these are non-weight-bearing placements.

My head, neck, shoulders and spine are all in alignment and his head rests off-centre at my shoulder. This isn't a position for him to be in for too long, as although I'm aligned, he isn't. This tends to be a hold for when they're awake and can participate with their upper body. Ideally, in the passive hold, you'd be using one arm under their bum and the other to support the upper back and neck.

In the next picture I'm supporting Izzy at her bum with my right hand and on her upper back with my left hand. She's nearly 3 weeks old here but was born 4 weeks early, so is very much a tiny newborn and is very light. I'm fine supporting her weight with my hand until I start getting signals of muscle fatigue. For people with hand and/or wrist issues, using your forearm is a good place to start for working out an alternative means of support.

You may notice that my shoulders aren't in symmetrical alignment here, and this is where pictures sometimes don't tell the whole story. At first glance it may look like my left shoulder has dropped, but it's actually my right shoulder that's *lifted*, as I'm bearing her weight, adjusting to her wriggles and lifting her a little higher on my chest. Adjustments like this are normal.

As you can see, she's in the reflexive spread-squat position at the normal and natural angle for her body. Her feet press into my abdominal area (handy if you have more than a little body fat here!), providing an "anchoring" point, but I'm bearing her weight.

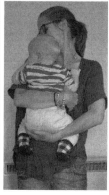

Passive - misaligned

By creating a "shelf" with my stomach, I'm creating undue pressure on my lower spine, compressing the vertebrae. I'm also creating downward pressure on the internal organs in my abdominal area and below. This presents a bigger problem if you have prolapse and/or diastasis recti. If I do this when they're awake, I'm also conditioning my baby to think that s/he can do nothing to participate, as I've eliminated the need for them to actively try to hold on. So nobody wins here.

My arms also bear weight in a different way – there's a pulling motion from my shoulders downwards if I let any weight rest against my arms or a tensing action if I pull him in tight against my body.

With Gina, she's bearing weight with her hand rather than her forearm. This isn't presenting a problem quite yet as she's using her other arm to hold him in tight, so that arm is doing most of the work. It will become a problem if he's held like this for any length of time. She's also leaning back to counter him being on her front.

By changing how and where we're holding we can create more comfortable and sturdier-feeling support. For me, I can use one forearm to hold Isaac from knee-pit to knee-pit and use my other arm and hand to support his upper back. If I do this he will be fully supported and I won't need to lean back to use my body to help me.

For Gina, she can also use her forearm to support James from knee-pit to knee-pit. If she does this she can let more of his weight rest on her arm, meaning she doesn't need to squeeze him into her so tight further up. She can continue to use her other arm to support his upper body, but it can act more like a barrier. Again, she will then not need to use her body as a bracing point.

Active - aligned

Aligned, active front carrying comes in the form of active clinging with the lower extremities. Depending where on the body they're supported, they will either participate more with their upper body or lower body. It can also be fully supporting the lower body, leaving them to do the rest of the work with their upper body.

In this example, I'm supporting Isaac at his lumbar spine. He uses his legs to cling onto me, and his left arm to hold onto my right arm. He's looking to his right, turning his body in that direction, so he's also using my forearm to his advantage by leaning back on it. Because of his backward lean I've placed my hand and fingers around his side to hold him better.

If he were facing me he would likely use both arms to hold on (usually one on my arm and the other on my shoulder) and I would simply support him with my forearm placed further round his body so my hand clears it, resting loose in the air.

Active – misaligned

Although James is supporting his upper body here, Gina is bending backwards to feel better balanced – almost as if to avoid tipping over, as James is creating distance between their bodies.

She could align her body, having her other hand ready just behind his back in case he becomes unbalanced from her adjustments. Doing this would likely make James feel less stable and encourage him to adjust his position too, so he sits more comfortably.

Another option, of course, is to change how she supports him so that she feels more balanced.

High off-centre carry (shoulder hug)

The big risk with this one is leaning backwards with your shoulder and upper back on the side you're carrying. It can be instinctive to lean back to support the baby better, but if you need to do this then they either aren't able to support their weight well enough and/or you're not providing the support they need. If the correct support is in place, or they are able to support themselves, there is no need (therefore no instinctive bracing reaction) to lean backwards.

Passive - misaligned

In this picture I'm rib-thrusting, and compensating for my backwards lean by holding my head forwards. I'm taking work away from my arm and using my body to bear most of it. Young babies and older babies/children who are asleep will require extra support and this is very much possible without using your body to brace them. Using our arms to do the work eliminates the need to create bracing points.

When you lean backwards at the upper back and add weight to it from the front you're creating undue strain on the muscles of the upper back and performing a compression action down to the lower spine.

You also need to be aware of what your shoulder is doing on the side their body is. Are you leaning your shoulder back as well as your spine?

With this carry you're looking to align your shoulders, and only use your shoulder as a kind of pillow for your baby or child to rest their head on. You will also need to make sure you're not using your ribs as a shelf.

Due to the positioning of this carry, they don't have an ergonomical body part to cling on to – one knee will be near the middle of your body and the other near or at your side. This makes the position inherently more of a passive one but it's still possible for them to cling on with their upper body.

With small babies they're able to keep their knees up as they have room on your body. They may not always sit in a deep squat though, especially when awake. This tends to be a more chair-like position for awake and active babies of most ages, and bigger babies/children with a lack of room. They also may sit with knees more in line with hips, depending on how you're holding them and/or their preferences.

The way to fully support them with an aligned body in this carry is to use your arm or arms to bear their weight. Remember to seat their bum in the middle of your forearm rather than directly on the wrist.

Smaller babies can be held closer to your elbow if preferred. The support in stabilising the body with your upper arm can work really well.

For alignment with this carry we're looking to once again stack our head, neck, shoulders, ribs, pelvis and feet, and use our arms to do most of the work. It's possible – as mentioned – to use your shoulder to bear the weight of their head, which can help with upper-body support if you're not supporting them with your other arm.

Passive – aligned

This sort of carry tends to be handy for when they're asleep or tired in-arms, as well as for babies with reflux. As you can see, the shape of my upper body helps with keeping a curve in Isaac's spine even though I'm standing aligned and not bending my upper back. James is awake, and Gina supports his lower body with her forearm and his upper back with her other hand.

Less weight is borne by your arm at their legs when they're draped over your shoulder as Isaac is. This means that his less-than-optimal looking leg position (knees a little lower than hips) isn't such an issue as my shoulder is bearing much of his weight.

Active – aligned

Active shoulder hug carrying can look similar to passive holding when they're asleep, as they can use their body to lean on you in various ways. Here, Isaac's holding onto my left shoulder with one arm and leaning his body into my right shoulder. As you can see, the way they sit on this part of the body when active can be less-than-optimal too. This tends to happen more when they're older and we're less likely to use this as a regular carrying position.

Active - misaligned

Here I'm bending backwards at my upper back. It's a little hard to see because of my baggy top hiding the visual effect of the movement. This is creating a bracing point as Isaac sits up straight. He's using his torso to hold himself upright and doesn't hold on with his hands or arms. He's also extending his legs even further, making him basically pinned to my ribs with his legs.

This carry tends to work best with smaller babies. It's also a good one for when older babies and children are asleep, as you're able to adjust how and where you're holding and where their weight bears.

Facing out

This carrying position is a controversial one in the Western world of babywearing. Usual concerns include: over-stimulation, baby not being supported ergonomically and baby being "too young" to face out.

If we would just refer back to how we hold them in-arms, I think a lot of this concern would no longer exist. I think you'd be hard-pressed to find a baby who has never been held facing outwards in-arms. It's one of the natural carrying positions used with babies of different ages, even very young ones, and before they have upper body control – even full neck control!

It's important to note here though that carrying in-arms and in a sling can be *very* different when it comes to forwards facing. It tends to be the most different when it comes to babies of an age where they haven't gained full upper body control. Something I'd like to suggest as a way of bridging the gap between it being potentially unsafe carrying in a sling facing out and it being safe is to encourage in-arms carrying instead of saying "no, it's not possible".

Our arms are much better able to do the job than slings as we can provide the exact support needed. Not surprising, since our arms are part of us and slings are a man-made invention (no matter how long ago they were invented). Also, they provide a different kind of security to a sling.

With in-arms carrying it's much easier to support your baby exactly where is needed, even using your fingers to hold up a very wobbly head. You are also able to feel their breathing with the hand or forearm that's supporting their upper body. You're able to adjust their position (height, support etc.) in an instant and you get more sensory input. In short, carrying in-arms enables you to both support and monitor the baby well.

In a sling, babies without full trunk control need the same sort of support as those in-arms. This is much more difficult to replicate as a sling is an inanimate object and the points of support are limited by this. You also will not have as much feedback about how they're breathing. To gain a similar amount of support as provided in-arms, it would require the sling/carrier being tightened against the upper chest and neck, which would obviously restrict the airways. This is why babies facing outwards before they have neck and trunk control pull away from the wearer's body and seem to hang – adequate support cannot be achieved.

Facing outwards in-arms and in slings/carriers tends to work a lot better once trunk control is in place, as the support for their upper body comes from underneath the armpits. It's easy enough to support the thighs with a forearm and the chest below the armpits with the other forearm. With slings/carriers it's usually easy to create this support too, as it's not compromising their airways and the baby is able to balance themselves.
The over-stimulation concerns are certainly valid, especially as cues for this include detaching from the situation by "spacing out", which obviously is a hard one to catch when their face may not be easily visible.

One could argue that there are many times in each and every day where the earliest signals of over-stimulation (and many other areas of communication) aren't recognised and/or acted upon right away. We could also point out that with the baby on your body (in-arms or in a sling) you're at an advantage with proximity and bodily contact to notice and respond to those cues more rapidly.

With in-arms carrying, you're able to move baby to check on them more easily, and even in babywearing there are measures you can take such as having a clip-on or hand-held mirror to see their face. It's also important to pay closer attention to the 7 stages of consciousness so that the time spent statically facing outwards is when they are most content and alert.

When it comes to forward-facing positioning in babywearing, babies tend to be carried in one of two positions that are opposite ends of the spectrum. One is to have them hang with their legs down with their weight bearing on their crotch and/or thigh areas (this is seen in both narrow-base carriers and wider ones). The other is to mimic the internal-facing spread-squat position. Both of these are missing valuable insights from in-arms carrying.

If we look at how we carry in-arms in the forward facing position, we see that babies sit differently to how they do on the front, hip or back when facing in. The in-arms forward facing position tends to be knees in line with hips, and sitting at either a right angle or knees higher than bum, depending on their activeness at the time.

It's rare to see a baby carrier which mimics how they naturally sit in-arms. The narrow-based carriers and wider-based ones which don't mimic the spread-squat tend to keep the baby with their knees lower than their hips.

Mimicking the inward-facing spread-squat comes from the research showing this position to be optimal for developing hips. It makes perfect sense to err on the side of caution when making a carrying aid, but it would be interesting to see research conducted on the effects of carrying facing outwards in the knees-in-line-with-hips position, as well as with the knees lower than their hips, both in-arms and in carriers.

Aligned

For yourself, you're looking to keep your chest open, bearing the weight somewhere between the middle of your forearm and close to your elbow. Here I'm also using my hands to "hold" him, but this is very minimal as it's more of a hand placement as my forearms and upper arms are doing the actual weight bearing.

In the following pictures you can just about make out a different way of holding – still with him sat on my forearms but my hands are clasped together in between his legs. Again, my hands/wrists aren't weight-bearing. My arms are doing that and my hands are in a placement position.

Aligned (l) and misaligned (r)

In alignment, my head, neck, spine and hips are all stacked and my chest is open. Isaac's upper body is a little away from mine as I'm not bracing him to my chest. If I had a flat chest I would more easily be able to hold him closer to my body.

In misalignment, my hips are thrust forwards, creating a bracing point/"seat" for his bum on my abdomen. I'm also using my ribs to lean him against my chest.

It's much easier to support a younger baby with just one arm without compromising on our wrist/s. With older babies, we need to pay attention to where the weight of each of their thighs is bearing to find the most comfortable point to support them with our arm/s.

Hip carry

Hip carrying tends to be one of the easiest ways of carrying actively due to how well babies and children tend to "slot" onto the hip. It's interesting to note, however, that research looking into which ways of carrying loads would be most effective for humans came up with a negative correlation between hip carrying and energy expenditure. I spoke about this research in Chapter 2,[1] noting how the potential of increased energy expenditure could be useful if you want to use carrying as a form of intentional exercise.

The thing is, though, that all the load tests were of static masses. Even in the hip carrying test, a weighted mannequin was used. As you can see, this really isn't a good comparison to a human baby or child, even when it comes to passive carrying. We know that even in passive holds (and babywearing) the baby/child participates to a certain extent. The researchers seem to have overlooked the fact that human babies and children are *not* completely passive loads/dead weights.

This research has been used as an example as "proof" that

babywearing is better for/easier on our bodies than in-arms carrying due to the decreased energy expenditure seen in the weighted vest category. Obviously more research needs to be conducted to truly evaluate energy costs of actual carrying, but when research is limited we tend to look for the things closest to what we're talking about to back up our thoughts.

Of course, the same is obviously true for me with this book, and I'm sure that some of the correlations I've spotted will have their own flaws too!

As I noted earlier, it does seem that biologically female people tend to lean more towards hip carrying than biologically male people. I wonder if this could be rectified, even if to a lesser extent, by encouraging hip carrying for all. We know that babies adapt to the surface area provided (wider spread squat on front of body than hip) so surely, if another parent or carer has a wider hip area than the gestational parent, the baby should surely be able to work at least within its adaptation to the hip vs. front ratio of the gestational parent?

I would even stick my neck out further and suggest that they can adapt beyond this, knowing that baby- and child-rearing used to be a "village" process. Babies and children used to be passed around various members of the close-knit communities people used to live in. Surely their carrying behaviour was adapted to this? Another subject for research!

On the other hand, maybe certain types of carrying aren't for everyone? We know that as individuals we have our own preferences, so maybe this also extends further? It's definitely something that would be worth looking into further, especially seeing how babies adapt to different body types.

Now, let's take a look at hip carrying – both ergonomically and otherwise.

Hip carrying can begin from whenever you feel the right time is for you and your baby. The smaller they are, the more awkward it tends to be, both because of their size and the level of bodily support needed.

Hip carrying tends to work well from when they're sitting unaided, or a little before. It definitely can work at a younger age, and I find the caregivers who hip carry from younger find their special ways of adapting based on their unique dyad. We're going to look at it from 6 month onwards here.

Passive – aligned

Aligned, passive hip carrying requires at least full support for the lower limbs. If the baby isn't sitting unaided yet, they will need some form of support for the upper body too. The degree of this support will vary depending on their stage of development.

A slight adjustment to compensate for the changed centre of gravity will likely be needed, mainly if standing still. When walking, the movement of our hips tends to mean we need less adjustment as the fluidity of the carrying process as a movement seems to work in harmony with walking.

Passive hip carrying tends to be higher than active hip carrying. This is because they need to be higher up on your body to get the right leverage with your arm to carrying them more effectively and efficiently. It also requires your elbow to help with knee lift on one side and your hand for knee lift on the other side. Their weight should bear roughly in the middle of your forearm through their bum.

Of course, with older babies and children there's work being done with the upper body to hold them up and maintain balance. The idea here is to take away their need to cling with the lower extremities. They're also able to make this position more passive by leaning into your upper body and shoulder.

Passive – misaligned

Passive hip carrying without full support for their legs tends to require a firm grip with the arm as it's harder to bear their weight if they're further away from your body.

Babies and children not used to clinging onto the body tend to drop one or both of their legs, and this results in the addition of a hand needing to be placed in or near the knee pit to "hoik" it up.

Misaligned passive hip carrying tends to involve using the ribs and/or abdomen to brace them on our body. We may lean to the opposite side we're carrying on to do this.

Ways of holding comfortably in a passive hold here are:

- Provide a solid base of support for bum and legs, from knee pit to knee pit
- Resist sticking your hip out to the side beyond the most basic of postural adjustment – use your arms not your body
- Use an arm to support their upper body if need be
- Avoid twisting your spine to provide upper body support with your opposite arm
- Switch sides regularly to give your muscles a break

In active hip carrying we support the baby or child on their spine at armpit level or lower down on their back. Supporting higher up means they have to do more work with their legs to cling on. Lower support gives more freedom of movement for their torso.

Adjust your support, first based on their stage of development. Before they're sitting well unaided, the ideal place for support is under the armpits. This can be swapped up with lower support to encourage the development of upper body control, but pay attention to how well they respond to it and go with their needs. Also remember that the support should just be "there" rather than creating pressure on the spine by pulling them in towards you.

Once that sturdy torso control is there you may find you support them lower down more often as they want to practice this new skill.

Once they're walking unaided you should have much more flexibility with how and where you support them, as their overall strength increases that much more. You will likely find that they have their own preferences though!

Active – aligned

Aligned, active hip carrying requires you to resist the urge to hip thrust. It may feel like you have the urge more when you're providing little support for them, but it tends to be partially a trust issue. We need to trust them to cling and to trust that our body is providing the perfect place for them to sit.

There will likely be a slight adjustment to the side you're carrying on, because of adjusting to your new, combined, centre of gravity, as well as compensating a little for any backwards lean from your baby/child, but this should be minimal. Remember to make adjustments from your spine and then follow through by shifting your weight from your upper body over to the side you're carrying on.

Active – misaligned

We may slip into passive carrying behaviours even during active carrying by once again sticking our hip out. Being aware of if and when you do this will help you notice what's triggering it. This hip thrusting is our way of creating a bigger ledge/seat for them to sit on. It hinders active carrying as you end up bracing them onto the hip meaning their leg/s tends to drop.

You can see this here, where I'm using my other hand to prop his knee up. He's still sturdy and active in his upper body and isn't relying on me fully for support, but his lower body realises he doesn't need to do much now because my movement has sent the message to him that I'm taking over the work.

Back carry

Back carrying tends to be something we do with older children in-arms. This is because of the limited range of motion our arms have when bringing them behind our bodies, as well as the need for strong clinging behaviour and stability from the person we're carrying.

Research into carrying loads on our backs has provided useful insights, such as how they may affect our spine. Something I found sparked a curiosity in me about how we compensate for weight on our backs. There was a research study conducted with internally framed and externally framed backpacks, looking at how body posture compensated for the weight while standing still.[2]

The results showed that there was a forward displacement of the upper body, hips and knees. I looked into this further when comparing it to carrying and realised that it's actually needed sometimes. We can't support them in the same way on our back as we can on our front so there may be some postural adjustment. The key is to stay aligned and pivot from the hips rather than bend over, and to keep a slight bend in the knees to protect the joints.

As an aside, something thrown up from this study baffled me! It showed that the women overwhelmingly preferred externally framed packs, and men the internally framed ones. Internally framed packs have the metal frame inside the backpack, and the externally framed ones are on the outside. If I'd hazarded a guess, I would have gone with the opposite preferences, as internal-framed packs hug the wearer whereas external-framed ones create a gap between the pack and the person's back.

Interestingly, internal ones are more stable and external ones not so stable. It makes me wonder if there's a biological difference when it comes to back carrying, in that biologically female bodies may be designed to be more responsive to less stable loads. It's something to think about for sure.

It is important to note though, that this was a very small study. It's more what came up for me to muse on than thinking there's a strong correlation.

In-arms carrying on the back will usually require the caregiver to use one or both arms to partially support the baby/child. The big risks of injury with back carrying come from over-extending the ligaments of the shoulders, weight-bearing around the wrist area and hunching over to counter their weight.

Let's look at aligned and misaligned back carrying:

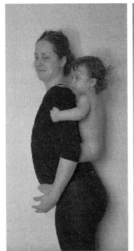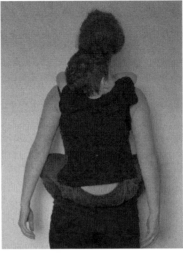

Active – aligned

Here are some examples of fully active back carrying. Isaac is 20 months here and has the strength to hold on independently. However, his legs are only just long enough to hook his knees round my waist so he doesn't quite have the leverage he needs to make it easier for *him*. This means I need to adjust my body to help him. What I'm doing here is pivoting from my hips. I keep my head, neck and spine aligned whilst pivoting forwards – this keeps my back protected.

Isaac clings on strongly with his legs and curves his feet in towards my body for better holding. He uses his arms and hands to hold onto my arms tightly.

With Logan, I'm able to stand completely straight. He's much taller and is able to use his legs to wrap around my waist, resting his feet at the front of my body, and hook his arms over my shoulders. There's no need for me to help him until he begins to tire.

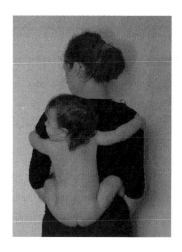

Active – misaligned

Here's an example of misalignment. Isaac's sitting off-centre on my back and I'm countering this by sticking my left hip up, dropping the other side of my body, and leaning forwards. To correct this I can use my arms to move him to the middle of my back and whilst I'm holding him I can align my hips, spine and head.

"Passive" back carrying is still fairly active, as they still have to use their upper body to stay upright and to hold on. A truly passive back carry would mean leaning forwards enough so they're effectively laying against your back. It's incredibly hard to use an arm to support their upper back when they're on your back.

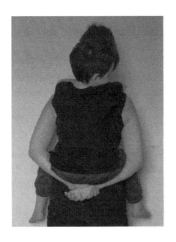

Passive - aligned

Here I'm supporting Logan's lower body. Although my hands are clasped, his weight is bearing on my forearms through his thighs, rather than down by my wrists and hands. My hands are merely together, to keep them from dangling. Logan steadies his upper body by wrapping his arms over my shoulders and holding his hands in front of my neck.

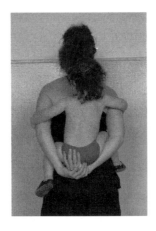

Passive – misaligned

Here I'm using my hands and wrists to bear Isaac's weight. I'm risking injury and won't be able to carry this way for long. I'm also dragging my shoulders down, so there's strain on my shoulder ligaments too. Isaac holds onto my arms with his hands to stabilise his upper body.

Shoulder carry

In shoulder carrying there's a certain degree of forward-leaning of the head and neck. This is to create the space to accommodate the baby or child's torso behind your head and for them to adapt their balance to how they're seated. The key to keeping this carry comfortable and limiting negative impact on the cervical and thoracic spine is to use pivoting actions. This creates a strong platform for any bracing weight, and stabilises the spine.

At the neck, have a feel for the top of the thoracic spine. This is a noticeably larger vertebra at the bottom of your neck. This is the T1 vertebra. Above this you should be able to feel the much narrower vertebrae of the cervical spine. Now, put the pads of your forefinger, middle finger and index finger just above the T1 vertebra, pressing just enough to just about feel approximately C7-C4 of the cervical vertebrae.

Once you've located these, nod your head and feel the movement of the cervical spine. The vertebra will push back against your fingers and a forward facing curve will present. Next, realign your neck and place your fingers back to the same position. This time, pivot your head from the neck. You should feel an opposite reaction – the cervical spine moves away and a slight "dip" in the muscles of the neck should be felt.

If you have the range of motion needed in your arm/s, you can test this with the thoracic spine too. Placing your hand or fingers on the spine either between the shoulder blades or just below and repeating the flexion motion by hunching the shoulders forwards will enable you to feel the forward curve created by this motion.

The stacking of the vertebrae creates a strong base for weight to bear on. Misaligning your spine creates weak spots and increases the risk of injury, as the discs aren't positioned correctly to cushion the bones.

There may also be a need for a little forward lean of the torso to bring about better balance for you. If this is needed, remember to keep the spine aligned and pivot from the hips.

Let's see how this looks in carrying:

Active – aligned

Both Tom and I are keeping our shoulders aligned and our heads pivot forward, keeping our cervical spinal vertebrae and discs in alignment.

Shoulder carries are suitable from when the baby has very good torso control and actively knows how to use their arms to hold onto your head or holds onto your hands well when they're up there. You will also need to work out how much support you're able to provide and whether this tallies up with where they are developmentally.

Even if they're able to hold on well with their arms and stabilise their torso, their legs may be too short to provide a weighted hinging action and leverage. In this case you would need to support their legs to prevent their weight from sending them backwards, or pull them forwards while holding their hands.

Active carrying here requires advanced clinging capabilities from a younger child. The bigger they get the easier it becomes for them to support themselves fully in this sort of carry.

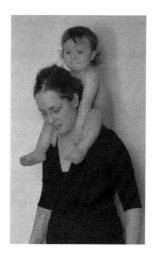

Active – misaligned

Here my neck is bent forwards and downwards, rather than pivoting. I've dropped my shoulders and rounded my upper spine too.

To correct this I need to get my shoulders, spine and neck back into alignment. I would need to at least hold Isaac's legs to steady him as I make my adjustments. It can be tricky to do adjustments safely in this carry, so if anything feels difficult to do or unstable, you may want to take them down and start again.

Passive – aligned

Aligned, passive, shoulder carrying follows the same principles as for active shoulder carrying. A pivoting motion of the head to keep the neck aligned, and a neutral spine from the thoracic downwards.

Passive – misaligned

Here I'm leaning forwards at my upper back, rounding my thoracic spine. I've also tipped my head down slightly so my neck isn't aligned. This will result in a sore back and neck for me.

In the earlier days you'll find they tend to grab on quite tight to your head (or hair or neck!) in an active carry. As they get older and stronger they'll need to hold on less with their arms and should use their hands/arms more for stabilising themselves from the movement created by you walking.

They also vary in whether they want to participate or not, and when they don't they tend to curve their spine and rest their weight on the back of your head and neck. This can obviously be very uncomfortable for you, and awareness is needed when this happens - providing additional support or changing the carry may be needed.

Just the beginning

As you can see, there are many different considerations for each way of carrying, and these change as they get older and/or stronger, as well as when they're tired or sleeping. These are the basics and should help you to begin to understand how ours and our children's bodies work in carrying.

There's so much to discuss when it comes to each way of carrying and so many different quirks within dyads, which is better explained visually and kinetically. This is why I prefer to teach in-person or through video – nothing beats a hands-on approach!

As with so many things, knowing the basics and using your own lived experience to tailor it to your needs tends to work well. Getting to know your baby/child's unique carrying behaviours as well as your own will help you to adjust and adapt accordingly.

Alignment and comfort checklist

- Is my body in alignment before I pick them up?
- What's my alignment like now they're in arms?
- Where can I feel their weight bearing? Is it on my body? Arms? In muscles or ligaments?
- Where do I need to provide support and how does this affect my body?
- Am I balanced well? If not, what do I need to do to shift my weight in the direction of my new centre of gravity?

Chapter 12

Encouraging Clinging Behaviour

We've looked at several different active and passive positions to see the differences in how babies and children become engaged or disengaged in the carrying process. Next up is thinking about ways in which we can encourage clinging behaviour. Lots of things can affect this, positively and negatively.

Some things are to do with their own abilities, which will also depend on the baby/child's stage of development, previous history of being carried, physical skill etc. Other things are environmental. Just like any other area of development, nature (genes) plays a big part in the capabilities of a baby or child. Nurture (environment) can elicit wonderful results even when genetics aren't favourable, but can only help to a certain extent.

There are lots of things we can do to encourage clinging behaviour, and some may work better than others. It's all going to be individual to your child. We have a bunch of options, but every child (and every caregiver, for that matter) is different. There will never be a one-size-fits-all approach. Try different things out and go with what you and your baby/child respond to best. You'll probably even work out other things you can do that are immeasurably tailored to your carrying dyad, which is fantastic!

Those who have been carried in slings/carriers which mimic the physiological in-arms positioning will be more used to the position than those who haven't. They will also be used to the positional and balancing micro– and macro-adaptations that come with being in a sling/carrier that has some wiggle room. This gives them a stronger chance of them having laid down some of the foundations needed for active in-arms carrying. Babywearing can support the in-arms process and is a great alternative for when you may need your arms, need to conserve some energy, or just want them to sleep already!

Babies used to spending time in prams may have less of a foundation to work with, and those who spend a lot of time in prams/car seats/baby chairs/bouncers etc. may need more help. It all really depends on their day-to-day range of movement, how they're being carried in-arms already, and their predispositions. Just like any area of development, some babies/children do things faster and some have stronger tendencies towards certain behaviours, and others are more resilient to sub-optimal practices.

For example, if you practice Elimination Communication with your baby, or if you potty train a child, they may be very much inclined to stay dry all the time, but another baby may not prioritise eliminating away from their body over playing. It doesn't necessarily mean you are doing anything better/wrong, just that babies and children are as individual as adults. We all have different areas of interest, different areas in which we excel, and babies are no different.

Wherever they're at, you can encourage clinging behaviour and teach them to be active participants for lengths of time suited to them personally. We'll take a look at what can help or hinder carrying, and then focus on different age ranges and what things you can do that may help them.

Things which help clinging behaviour

Carrying skin-to-skin is a fantastic way of nurturing the clinging instinct. With no barrier between yours and their skin, the sensory input isn't hindered and you both benefit from the grip that comes from the friction of skin-on-skin. This is biologically the perfect in-arms carrying setup.

Finding time to carry skin-to-skin (with baby/child either naked or with just a nappy/underpants on) will benefit you both in lots of ways. Learning will come more easily through full sensory stimulation via the skin as well as the added grip, but also the general skin-to-skin benefits can be achieved.

It may seem daunting at first to think about how you can carve out this time in your day-to-day life, especially if you're busy, but it really doesn't need to be hard. Here are some examples of ways you can bring more skin-to-skin carrying into your lives without having to carve out extra time:

- Stripping them off as soon as you run a bath for them – you could try doing whatever you do whilst the bath is running while holding them in-arms
- After you've had a bath or shower – dry off and have a quick hold whilst you grab your clothes
- Dancing in your underwear – if you're a household that enjoys dancing together, why not incorporate some skin-to-skin carrying with a fun activity?
- When they're ill – this goes without saying, we know the great benefits of skin-to-skin contact with regards to stabilising temperature, so the next time they're ill, consider carrying them around the house skin-to-skin
- Sharing a shower – this is a really easy one if they need a rinse down!

Carrying on the beach, especially going for a (barefoot!) walk is a great way to experience skin-to-skin contact in warmer weather if you wear a bikini/bikini top/crop top/no top. Swim shorts and bikini bottoms work well as limited clothing on your lower half. The baby/child will need at least bare legs, and preferably a naked torso for better sensory input.

The same for nature walks etc. - if you're able to provide some bare skin (at least around your waist, and their legs bare at least from the knee down), you will both benefit from the biologically normal carrying response. Skin-to-skin out in nature is the best of both worlds!

Lots of the time, though, we need to wear clothes. Whether it's because it's a cold time of year or we're outside of the house, it doesn't mean that it's time to throw in the towel. There are ways to carry skin-to-skin in-arms even if you need outer clothing. You can use things like an oversized cardigan or hoodie, a bathrobe or dressing gown, or a large blanket to wrap around you both.

There may also be times where they're able to wear less clothes and you may either need or want to wear something. This can work well too.

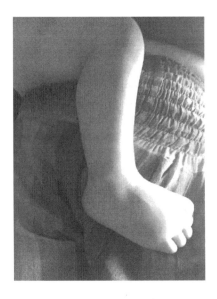

There are also different fabrics which make it easier for your baby/child to hold on to you. The sensory stimulation is dulled but the practice is still there.

Types of clothing which help with carrying include:

- Fabrics which promote gripping (e.g. 100% cotton)
- Clothes which allow full range of motion for the baby/child

- Non-restrictive clothes for you too

Clothes which aren't as grippy can still work, making them work harder to hold on without being too much work to be doable. For example, my boys prefer to wear joggers in the cooler weather, and all through winter. These tend to be fairly smooth, but as long as I'm wearing something with a bit of grip it works. If I'm wearing my fleece coat, not so much.

If slippery clothes are unavoidable out of the house you may need to revert to more passive carries.

In water

Carrying skin-to-skin then going into a body of water or a shower seems to create a sort of suction seal, which keeps them gripped on you amazingly well. Also, the sensation of water on the skin seems to trigger a tighter gripping response. What a great survival mechanism! However, holding a wet baby against a wet body hinders the process as you're both slippery.

Taking your baby/child into the shower with you is a great way of spending time carrying in-arms, skin-to-skin, whilst bathing them. Always helpful to combine activities! Trying to shower yourself can be a bit tricky with them in-arms (but doable if you want to!), so you may want someone on hand to take them once they're washed.

Carrying in a swimming pool is also a good way to feel what's going on where, with less of a burden. The "weightless" feeling and better range of motion of your body can also help with working out postural adjustments.

Things which hinder clinging behaviour

Any excess bulk between the legs, such as some types of cloth nappy, makes it difficult for babies to hold on. Winter coats can make things more difficult too. Whatever bulk there is creates distance from their body and yours, and can alter the natural position and motion of their body.

Nappy-free time is a good thing for babies, full stop. It gives them time to use their normal range of bodily motion, and can help with carrying around the house. If you're not aware of natural infant hygiene/elimination communication, the idea of carrying a nappy-free baby might seem quite a scary thought!

Don't worry though. Young babies who are held in a physiologically normal way, on the body and facing the person carrying them, rarely urinate or defecate without good warning. Even older babies and children who are used to going in a nappy can still retain the ability to give non-verbal signals when being carried.

If you're worried, try carrying skin-to-skin after a nappy change. For good measure, just hold your baby over the toilet in a spread-squat position and let them know they can try and pee/poo (you can make a "pssss, pssss" or another sound if you want), and see if they go. If they do (and this seems to happen more often than not on a first go), bonus! You now have extra time to not think about them eliminating on you!

Restrictive clothing (e.g. denim) hinders the range of motion and comfort for the baby/child. Restrictive/uncomfortable clothing can make carrying harder for you too. Think about how you tend to choose the type of clothing you wear based on the activity you're doing. What would you wear for gardening? Doing some sort of exercise? Carrying requires freedom of movement and an accessible "clinging point". It also needs to be comfortable for you. Things like belts and tight/stiff waistbands don't do anyone any favours. Pressure points aren't fun for anyone.

Slippery fabrics make it very difficult for babies and children to hold on, even if they're trying hard and have great clinging abilities.

Providing lots of support will also hinder clinging behaviour as they will become used to you doing most or all of the work. If they get used to passive carrying, even if they're used to sitting in a spread-squat position you'll find one or both knees gravitate downwards, meaning you get into a vicious cycle of having to use a hand to prop it up, or a hand and elbow if both. If they do this, you can keep adjusting their pelvic tilt so their knees are higher up and provide less support lower down so they build up their clinging capacity.

Younger babies

Working with their reflexes is a great starting point. Pay attention to the reflexive adjustments they make when you carry them. Be aware of whether or not you're compensating for the added load by rib– or hip-thrusting. Catch yourself before these become carrying habits.

Notice how they sit on you and engage (or not!) in the carrying process in different positions. Notice also how these behaviours change with any postural adjustment you make. How do they behave when you bend or reach to grab something? What about when you turn suddenly? These will all provide clues as to their current clinging abilities and highlight where and when they may need extra support.

As your baby gets stronger, notice the different ways in which you need to provide support for them. Be aware of how they're practicing supporting their body in different ways. As you adjust your support, what's happening with the areas of their body that you're not supporting? Learn to notice their in-arms tired cues so you can respond promptly.

If you use a sling/carrier, start noticing how you're holding your body with this static load. How's your posture? Are you aligned, or making compensations for your baby/child? How is your sling/carrier fitted to you? Is it tightened correctly? If there's slack, how is your body compensating for it and how are they compensating posturally?* Is it over-tightened? If so, how is it affecting their positioning and your posture? Do you hold your body differently when they're on the front or the back? If you hip carry, what's your body doing then?

Note: it's perfectly normal to need some slack when baby is awake and active, so they can move around more and not be pinned to your body - the key is working out how much you're personally able to manage without it affecting your posture and their clinging capabilities.

Older babies

One of the simplest things is aligning your body. If you're carrying them on your hip, don't give them a "shelf". If you're carrying them on your front, don't give them one either! If you're carrying on your back, don't overcompensate by sticking your bum out.

Use your arm/s to adjust how much support you're giving. Use more support as they tire, and encourage them to sit in a more passive position (knees higher up, spine curved) so they're leaning into you and are closer to your line of gravity.
Support them on different parts of their body to encourage them to work different muscles and for you to bear more or less of their weight. This enables them and you to cycle the muscle groups you're using, enabling longer and more comfortable carrying.

Pay attention to their cues. If they're trying to look at something or are pointing something out to you, maybe a position change is needed? If they're physically disengaging (straightening legs), it's time to move to a passive position or for them to get down and roam free. They may just need a run around, a short break, or they may be ready for sleep.

That's the beauty with in-arms carrying - the physical and vocal cues enable frequent changes of position, plus you're also in control of changing position if *you* need to, based on what your body is telling you.

Children

Making parts of carrying into a game can help with encouraging their participation. You're also better able to describe what you need them to do and why (although still do this with younger babies!), and them respond in a way you're hoping for.

Children tend to want to be carried when they're tired of walking, which isn't a great starting point for encouraging them to do more work! Carrying them for short periods of time when they're happy and have energy can lay down the foundation for easier carrying when they're tired.

Playing games you wouldn't associate with carrying can help their clinging capabilities. For example:

- Playing "horses"
- Pretending to be asleep so they climb on your back, and then rearing up
- Climbing activities (trees, indoor climbing walls etc.)
- Have them lie down on the floor, get on your hands and knees above them, then lower your body down and have them grab onto you with their arms and legs. See how long they can hold on as you crawl around the room!
- Encourage clinging and climbing behaviours in play. For example get them hanging on bars at the park (and you join in too if possible!), using climbing nets and zipwires etc.

It can be easier in some ways to encourage clinging behaviour in children, as you can explain to them what to do and they're likely to understand on a deeper level. Things like "I need you to hold onto me", "Your legs need to be higher", "Try holding onto me more with your arms" etc. are simple but effective instructions.

When you give piggybacks, try providing less support. This will teach them what they need to do with their arms and legs to hold on. Eventually you should be able to provide minimal support with one or both arms until they're tired.

Babywearing

Using certain baby slings/carriers can help with in-arms carrying. Ones which hold the baby/child in the spread-squat position keep them used to the physiological carrying position, so they are more likely to automatically adopt it in-arms. For older babies/children just getting started with this sort of sling/carrier will help them get used to being held in this way whilst you build up your carrying stamina.

Babywearing is usually less active than some "passive" in-arms positions, and can be completely passive at times (e.g. when asleep), but can still be active to a certain extent. When the baby/child is awake and active, allowing enough wiggle-room will enable them to engage their upper body more. When they're at this stage of awareness you don't need to have them completely melded to your body, as you would if they were asleep or tired.

Using carries which support their body less and require them to hold on more is also something worth considering. You can find your local sling library or Babywearing Consultant to advise you on this.[1]

You may find that as you encourage their clinging behaviour they may want to be carried more. This is completely natural, just like if they enjoy slings they'll want to spend time in them. It's a normal part of daily movement for you both and forms part of their daily dose of attachment. Being held is an important part of their development, and the fact they need us to transport them until they can do so independently supports the want for regular carrying.

It can be frustrating at times when all our babies seem to want is us, especially if we feel we're being pulled away from other things we need or want to do. Far from being "clingy", this behaviour is completely normal, and is laying the foundation for their independence as they grow older. The first year or two can be especially full-on, but know that you're actively encouraging their secure attachment.

What does clinging behaviour evolve into?

So what comes next? What happens once they're out of the in-arms phase? What happens once they're even older and barely carried at all? Well, clinging behaviour is linked to many things. It provides the foundations for other areas of physical development as well as having its own "end game".

When your baby is pulling themselves up, they're using their hands to pull up and steady themselves. They use their feet to balance, and toes to grip and balance. The plantar grasp and Babinski's sign are key to this, and, as we know, these reflexes integrate once they're walking well.

When they start climbing, they use their hands to pull and hold on, and feet, knees and legs to climb, grip and balance. This develops into being able to climb ladders, trees, even doorframes!

When nurtured, it enables us to keep strength and the ability to cling for longer periods with our inner thighs and calves, as well as hands and feet. This of course means enabling children to have active childhoods with lots of freedom of movement.

The natural sitting-spread-squat (the biologically normal sitting position on another's body), as we know, is one of the steps along the way to a standing squat. A "full squat" or, what I call a "passive squat", requires the person to squat to below knee level. This can, of course, be done knees in line with hips, but is easier to elicit with wider-stance legs. Ensuring the ability to squat remains will help immensely with overall muscular health and posture.

Squatting keeps the psoas long and flexible, preventing tight hips and hamstrings, plus keeps the glutes strong. This all helps with our range of movement and overall strength. Carrying in a spread-squat position helps with regular practice of this range of motion and makes the transition to standing squats a very natural one, and a position they're likely to use more often as they've been used to it for so long.

It could be argued that we really don't need to encourage this biologically normal behaviour because we have all the conveniences of modern day life. Yes, it's true that many of us aren't required to have this range of motion and bodily strength, but the health implications are clear.

As adults, we can clearly benefit from the full range of clinging behaviours. I hope you agree that it's something we all need to be aware of to improve the health of the next generation.

Chapter 13

Your Comfort and Building Strength

So we've looked at the how's and why's, but what about if you apply all of this knowledge and find yourself experiencing discomfort, or you're struggling with the weight of carrying in-arms?

It's important for me to reiterate here that having a check-up with someone such as a doctor or physiotherapist, osteopath or chiropractor to make sure all is well with you is the best first step, to rule out any pre-existing issues, and access treatment for any problems. Many problems with pain and/or discomfort come from pre-existing postural and/or alignment issues, and/or pregnancy/postnatal issues.

Having an awareness of the condition of your body will make it easier to notice what things make carrying more or less comfortable. Knowing what things make certain conditions worse will keep you aware of habits you may have that perpetuate this, and enable you to work on and/or fix them.

No matter what stage of life we're at – babies, children, adolescents, adults, in the throes of early parenthood, middle age, or later in life – a strong, healthy body is incredibly important for overall good health. We need a healthy dose of movement and resistance "training" to function at an average level. Whether you're reading this book as a parent of carrying-age children or are reading based on curiosity or an interest in in-arms carrying, I cannot stress enough the need to carry on (or start) working on your body so that it functions, not even in an optimal, but in a normal way.

We're so far from normal here in the UK that information about what is normal for humans may feel like "optimal" and we may get comfortable in our own version of normal, believing that it's good enough. It can be scary to see how far away from normal we may be that believing that a true normal is a superhuman feat is more comfortable for us.

I *know* it's hard to hear this, and even harder to even think about implementing the work to get back to normal, let alone imagining actually achieving it, but *it is so important.* Even if you reach a decision that you cannot or will not work on your own health, please think about doing more for any children you may have now, in the future or work with. The real difference comes with making a positive impact on the generations ahead of us, even if we choose to let our health slide.

It's important to recognise though, that a lot of behaviours are learned, and this is definitely the case with posture. Children pick up how we do things and tend to mimic those behaviours. Even picking just one, two or a few things to work on yourself will set a better example for your child/ren.

Future generations can only truly benefit from people willing to take the steps to ensure they suffer less than we do. You may think you're but one person, and maybe you feel like you're "too far gone" or don't have the time and/or energy, but think of the domino effect.

Your comfort

It's important that you are comfortable when you carry. Carrying isn't meant to hurt – that would make carrying our children hard, and indicate that maybe it's something we shouldn't do! Unfortunately if we've not been using our bodies in biologically normal ways and/or we've not been carrying in-arms regularly then we're likely to experience some discomfort in the early days and weeks of doing more.

In an ideal world, we'd fix our problems first, and then start carrying afterwards, but that's unlikely to be a possibility for most people, seeing as the people most interested in carrying have babies or children. Of course, if you've been told not to lift/carry by your healthcare provider, that's a different story. In general though, we're not told to stop carrying. This means adapting and working on how we carry as we do it.

Once you have answers about posture, alignment and/or health, you can look at how you're holding. It's useful to ask someone to take pictures or video of you carrying for you (or someone else) to look back at and see how you're carrying versus how you *think* you're carrying. Remember what I said about how when I'm driving it's not until I've unconsciously moved out of alignment for a while that I tend to notice it. It's because we carry out many activities on a sort of autopilot, and if our go-to positioning is sub-optimal, that's what our body will do when we're not consciously working on changing it.

Try to make sure it's not posed pictures or video - out and about when you're not expecting it is best to get a true snapshot! Make note of any postural and/or alignment issues and work on them as you carry, and in general.

One issue with misalignment and bad posture is that we don't necessarily associate it with problems we have. For example, you may suffer with "unexplained" lower back pain, and have a posterior pelvic tilt. Did you think that may be causing the problem? When you're carrying, if you're exacerbating a postural issue which is actually linked to your unexplained pain, you may just think that it's the type of carrying rather than how you're holding yourself.

This is one potential link – always get any unexplained pain checked out by a health professional for diagnosis and advice going forwards.

You may think you can't carry in a certain way because of an ailment, but I would encourage you to go deeper with your understanding of the problem (if need be) before completely ruling out the possibility of carrying in certain ways. Even if carrying in a specific way is definitely out of the question, you may be able to work out your own adaptations.

Where possible, speak to your healthcare provider/s about it, and offer up avenues of discussion. For example, there's no harm in asking your physiotherapist (or other HCP) for a more in-depth explanation of your condition, what caused it (look for links from the cause – was it potentially preventable?), if they think that working on posture and alignment may help in any way, what they suggest for comfortable carrying, what you can do to build up strength in that area, and what you may need to avoid.

You may find that the person you're seeing doesn't have a whole-body approach to treatment and may dismiss your thoughts. While I respect the specialised knowledge of medical professionals, I also believe in both "alternative" (as in, traditional) knowledge and the intuitive powers we each have. Getting a second (or more) opinion is always an option, and especially important if you've noticed correlations in what impacts your condition for the better or worse.

It's also important to recognise exactly what the HCP's training has been – it's very easy to think that anyone with any medical qualification has the knowledge, training and experience to speak about other things outside their remit. You may want to consider requesting (or adding privately) more professionals to your care team if this is the case.

If you're experiencing discomfort or pain in your arms/shoulders/neck/back or anywhere else, pay attention to how you're using your arm/s, holding your head and the rest of your body. Remember to bear weight with your muscles, not your ligaments, and pay attention to what part of your arm is providing support.

It can be easy to bear weight on the wrong part of your arm, especially if you're in a rush. It tends to be that we support them lower down, towards our wrist, when we're not paying attention. You'll likely realise this soon enough when your lower arm and wrist start protesting! If you're bearing their weight in a passive carry, try to make sure their bum sits in the middle of your forearm rather than closer to your wrist. You should find it's easier and that your arm creates a more parallel "seat" than when they're further down.

If your discomfort is from muscle fatigue, make sure you're taking the time to gradually build up how often and how long you're carrying for in-arms. Also notice how often you're using active or passive positions, and switch up how you're carrying so that you're using different muscles and enabling tired ones enough rest time. Try to give both sides of your body equal (or as close to equal) carrying time as possible when hip carrying.

Building up strength and stamina comes over time. If you're starting out with a younger/lighter baby, it's going to be easier on your body than with an older/heavier baby or child. You can obviously build up upper-body strength through specific exercises, but the best way to build up the strength and stamina needed to carry your baby/child is by doing exactly that - carrying them! You'll be working the exact muscle groups needed and used in carrying by simply doing the intended activity.

Something to consider is your efficiency when carrying. To increase the time you can carry for (at this point in time, without building up muscular endurance) without tiring, you need to be consuming less energy. Here are some things which increase energy consumption, and examples of how to avoid them.

Forward head posture

This increases the force on the body, creating extra burden. It also changes rib alignment, making breathing harder, which also increases energy expenditure.[1]

Baby/child leaning away from your body

Back to physics again! The further away from your line of gravity a load is, the heavier it feels - just like forward head posture increases the effective weight of the head on the spine. The science of this is as follows:

t = torque
d = the distance between the mass
f = force

$$t = d \times f$$

Torque is how heavy your baby/child feels, distance is how far away from your line of gravity they (the "mass") are, and force is the weight of the baby and how the weight bears on your body.

If they are actively participating in carrying, this will bring down how heavy they feel. If they're doing this but are leaning away from your body (Isaac loves doing this!) then they will feel heavier than if they're actively clinging but cuddled into your body.

Shorter stride

We all have an optimum stride length which helps with efficiency of energy expenditure. A shorter stride increases expenditure, so lengthening your stride will save you energy. A longer-than-optimal stride is more efficient than a shorter one.[2]

Using the wrong muscles to propel your body

Efficient walking comes from using the gluteus muscles rather than the quadriceps as the primary muscle group. Other benefits from firing from your glutes include exercising your pelvic floor...and your glutes! Your knee joints are also protected as you're not effectively lifting your leg out in front of you and falling onto it. Using your glutes means you're pushing off the ground with one foot and gliding your other leg forwards (and repeat).

Working against your combined centre of gravity

The less stable you are, the more energy you consume. To carry more comfortably you must work with your new CoG. The more balanced you are, the less compensatory movements you have to make. Think about when you walk normally. Do you swing your arms at your sides at all? If you do, you're doing this to compensate for some degree of instability. So you're looking to keep energy costs down as much as possible.

For more advice on comfort, check out the troubleshooting chapter!

Building strength

Perceived strength isn't the be-all-end-all factor here. For example, my husband does heavy lifting at work, and is much stronger than me in general, but I can carry our children longer because I'm the one who's done it the most. His muscles have been trained to lift heavy for short periods of time, but mine have been trained to carry for longer. I've got the muscle stamina.....and he uses passive positions mostly, so isn't doing himself any favours!

I'm planning on starting weightlifting sometime soon. Funnily enough, it's not to get stronger for carrying (it will become clearer why not in a bit). So, during the process of deciding to start this form of exercise, I obviously did a bunch of research to work out if it's right for me, what sort of exercises to do etc.

The more I learned about heavy lifting, the more I saw similarities to the carrying process. I observed the importance of proper form in terms of posture and alignment, as well as learning that heavy lifting exercises are compound movements. I also learned that there are two types of muscle fibre - slow twitch and fast twitch. Slow twitch fibers are responsible for endurance, so in exercise terms, are what are responsible for you being able to lift low weight for higher repetitions or jog for an extended period of time. Fast twitch muscles have two types - A and B. Type A will enable you to perform a long sprint or carry something heavy over a longer distance. Type B is for short, explosive moves, such as lifting a very heavy weight.

Back to compound movements. These work several groups of muscles at the same time. They're more effective than isolated movements for building muscle as they use greater amounts of muscle fibre and are working more muscle groups. Think about it – if you want to build more muscle mass all over, it's more efficient to work more than one group at a time.

Carrying is a compound movement as it uses more than one muscle group. In fact, carrying is a series of different compound movements, as we don't carry in just one way. It's a compound exercise for both the person carrying and the person being held. Each of the different ways of carrying – and holding on – engages different muscles. It's an excellent form of exercise, and I'd even go so far as to say that, in my opinion, it's one of the best whole-body exercises you can do.

If you want to get stronger to carry for longer, the best exercise for that is, like I said, simply carrying. You can of course target specific muscles with different endurance exercises if you feel like you're weak in a specific area, but nothing will work all the muscles better than performing the exact movements used in carrying. You just gradually build up how long you carry for, enabling your muscles to get stronger and build up endurance.

If you haven't figured it out already, heavy lifting isn't going to help me with carrying my children because it develops the fast twitch muscles as opposed to the slow twitch ones that I use in carrying. I have plenty of muscle development in the slow twitch department!

Carrying specific injuries

There are certain injuries that can result from incorrect carrying, such as repetitive strain injury and changes to the spine.

From the NHS Choices website:

"Repetitive strain injury (RSI) is a general term used to describe the pain felt in muscles, nerves and tendons caused by repetitive movement and overuse"

This includes carrying out tasks with incorrect posture, and doing something without adequate periods of rest, so preventative measures would obviously include resting enough and carrying with good posture.

Symptoms include[3]:

- pain, aching or tenderness
- stiffness
- throbbing
- tingling or numbness
- weakness
- cramp

If you experience any of these you may want to get it checked by your doctor for further advice.

If you are concerned about your posture, or that carrying is affecting it in some way, it's a good idea to speak to a professional for assessment and advice going forwards.

How long we've been living in sub-optimal positions affects how long it will take to make permanent changes. Many of us will be working on changes for the rest of our lives. That can sound daunting, but please don't let that put you off. There are so many ways we can make even small changes day-to-day. This awareness of how we're holding our bodies (in general and carrying), how we're sitting, how we're moving etc., can create daily change without having to try and find extra time in the day to do it. Protecting our bodies is important - even more so if we have a pre-existing condition.

Chapter 14

Special Considerations

This book has covered carrying based on the normally developing baby or child, and caregivers with no health issues or risk factors. As you know, I'm not a medical professional so it's outside of my remit to suggest different carrying solutions for special circumstances based on my thoughts and ideas. I can, however, use my knowledge along with medical research to offer some ideas for certain situations. Again, please always consult with your healthcare provider before trying any of these out, so they can discuss with you whether or not it's appropriate for yours or your baby/child's situation.

Pregnancy

As we've touched on already, pregnancy is a time where special attention should be paid to the ever-changing body. If you are pregnant, it's of the utmost importance to listen to your body and not overdo it, as well as keeping alignment and posture at the forefront of your mind. There is much less room for error when ligaments are softer and more prone to over-extension.

In pregnancy, it's advised that this is not the time to take up a new form of exercise, so if you've got an older child and have done limited carrying and are thinking of carrying more often, please speak to your healthcare provider for advice.

If you're carrying on the front in the early weeks and months, it's important not to brace your child's weight on your abdomen. Although it may seem tempting to use your new "shelf", we know that this creates downward pressure, and the last thing you need is to be weakening your pelvic floor!

Be very careful when carrying on your hip too. The pelvis is an area prone to instability in pregnancy, and if you're out of alignment when carrying on the hip you're risking injury.

You may find it easier to mix up in-arms carrying with sling use. There are lots of options, including ones which don't have anything around your waist. Using a sling can help reduce some of the exertion of carrying and enable you to carry comfortably on your back, balancing out the additional weight on the front.

As the pregnancy progresses, the lumbar spine starts to curve more to bear the weight. At first glance this seems worrisome, as we know that creating excessive curves can result in injury when load-bearing, but the biologically female body is specially adapted for this adjustment in pregnancy. The size of the spinal joints of the lumbar vertebrae is much larger in biologically female bodies, which helps to bear a greater load.[1] Also, during late pregnancy there is a posterior displacement of your centre of gravity.[2] It is, however, important that the body is kept aligned so that the additional curve isn't made greater, and to bear in mind that this adaptation of the body is directly linked to the weight-bearing coming from *within* your body.

When it comes to carrying in pregnancy you may find you do try to curve your lower back more to stabilise your weight plus the weight of your older baby/child. If you find yourself doing this, remember to reset your posture, putting them down to do so if needed and starting over again.

Postnatal bodies

Another time for extra attention is in the days, weeks and months after birth. The postnatal body takes a long time to recover from pregnancy and birth, even if it feels like you've snapped back to feeling normal. Hormone levels can take around

5 months to reach pre-pregnancy levels, the uterus takes around 6 weeks to reach pre-pregnancy size, bleeding can last up to 6 weeks or more, and it can take weeks or months for other healing to occur. It took 9 months or so to grow your baby/ies, plus the impact of birth on top of that, so it makes sense that full recovery isn't immediate.

As our bodies tend not to ping right back into pre-pregnancy shape and size, we need to navigate holding our tiny new baby/ies whilst getting used to our postnatal body. Paying extra attention to posture and alignment will help protect your recovering body, as well as listening to what it tells you about how much you can endure. There's no point in overdoing it, especially when it may result in you needing to be off your feet for longer.

If you've had a caesarean section, please try as best as possible to let your body heal. I know that in this day and age this can be hard, especially if you have older children to look after. It's important to prioritise this because of how your recovery may impact on your body, as well as on how you're able to look after your baby and any other children.

It may feel like you're fine very soon after giving birth but the same is true for c-sections as for vaginal birth. We may feel on top of the world and like we're practically back to normal, but it only takes one time where we go with how great we feel for it to set us back again. Recovery can be deceptive and sometimes the first inkling you get that you've overdone it is when you're back at home.

C-section recovery is even more important to be careful with, as you will have had major abdominal surgery. Additional considerations are making sure that you're carrying your baby high enough to clear your wound (very easy in-arms) and that how you're carrying isn't creating downward pressure on it.

Birth trauma

Traumatic births can have a significant amount of physical and/or mental impact on the gestational parent, and mental trauma may also be present in their birth partner/s too. In the case of physical trauma, there may be a period of time where carrying may not be advised, and when it becomes okay to do so extra precautions may need to be made.

In the case of mental trauma, carrying may be something the caregiver/s instinctively wants to avoid, though you may feel the opposite, and find that lots of physical contact helps you with your recovery and bonding. It's wise to pay extra attention to what your body and mind can handle. Playing it safe in the early weeks and months may help your recovery in the long term. If you find that you're feeling averse to carrying your baby/ies, please seek medical advice. This can be a symptom of a post-partum mental health disorder. There are lots of organisations which specialise in both birth trauma and postnatal mental health.[3]

It's very important to be aware of how any injuries you may have sustained will impact on your ability to carry, and how carrying may affect the physical trauma. Working closely with your healthcare provider and asking carrying-specific questions will make it easier for you to assess what is right for you at any given point in time.

Postnatal physical disorders

If you have diastasis recti, pelvic organ prolapse (POP) or other pelvic floor issues, please seek medical advice regarding the impact of lifting on your body, as well as how to take steps to heal. I'd like to also recommend Katy Bowman's book *Diastasis Recti* as an alternative point of view, as I'm aware that there are question marks over the effectiveness of some approaches to treatment of this and pelvic floor issues.

It's very important to make sure you're not doing anything that will make your condition worse. Aligned carrying supports a normal, healthy body, but there may be additional precautions you need to take beyond the obvious ones.

Premature babies

Premature babies thrive on human touch. Multiple studies have been conducted on the effect of holding prems and much has been proven on the positive effects of them having bodily contact with their caregivers and other human beings. Much of this has been to do with skin-to-skin contact, but a lot of this can be transferred to carrying.

The findings showing that holding babies can regulate their heartbeat, improve oxygen saturation, and regulate their hormones can be easily replicated to in-arms carrying by mimicking the actions and/or environment when moving around.

For example, keeping your baby skin-to-skin when carrying will mean that they benefit from the advantages already discovered. Moving whilst holding them skin-to-skin may even promote previously undiscovered benefits. We know that movement on our part enables reactions from the baby to present themselves and aids their motor development. Obviously with very premature babies this may not be the primary focus and for a while there may be a need for more focus on skin-to-skin.

When you think about it, the aim of kangaroo care is to provide a similar environment to the womb. This has always involved movement from the gestational parent. To protect your fragile baby in an environment which is greatly different to the womb you will need to think of how best to adapt what you can offer them in a way that supports their need for extra precautions in handling. Your baby's healthcare providers will be able to advise you on the extra precautions specific to your baby.

One way of helping to mimic a womb-like environment is to use a carrying aid such as a kangaroo top[4] or a sling which mimics the enveloping hold of the uterus.

Depending on the carrying aid used, you may need to use one or both hands to contribute to the support provided to make mobile carrying safe. Always refer to the safety points for carrying, making sure their airways are clear and there are no fall or bump hazards. Even if your carrying aid enables hands-free carrying, bear in mind the benefits that your touch can add to their experience.

In the womb babies benefit from the human touch of the womb, warm amniotic fluid, nutrition on tap, regular movement, the heartbeat of the person carrying them, and auditory stimulation (albeit muffled) from the environment the gestational parent is in. Outside the womb we have to create an artificial womb, as close to the real thing as possible. As you can imagine, this is no mean feat – there's no way to make this identical, as it's not the real thing. However, we can think about ways in which we can replicate, as closely as possible, the normal conditions which are vital to a baby thriving in the womb.

This may mean coming up with a program of progression of stimulus as the baby/ies gain strength and can endure more "outside influence". Depending on the prematurity of your baby, you may be able to treat them more like a term newborn, or you may need to take extra precautions. As always, please refer to you healthcare team's advice. Let's explore this from the earliest of prematurity onwards.

Very premature babies' skin is extremely fragile and susceptible to the gentlest of stroking. This is a time for passive engagement with regards to movement. The benefits of the skin-to-skin contact are clear, and the fact that having lots of it throughout their stay in hospital improves their response to gentle touch when they're older[5] shows that holding our tiny babies is important for normal development.

In cases of extreme prematurity or medical fragility, it may not be possible to carry them. Holding them is definitely beneficial, we know, but still touch and containment holds have been shown to produce less behavioural stress and more quiet sleep in preterm infants.[6] This can serve as a way to build up to in-arms carrying. It's worth speaking to the healthcare providers involved in your baby's care for their input, whilst listening to your own instincts.

As your baby/ies become medically stable you'll find you're able to hold them more. You may find that they are missing some primitive reflexes, or have an abnormal response to them. This is common with premature babies (especially in extreme prematurity) but the closer they get to "term" the stronger and more complete the reflexes tend to get.[7]

To be clear, I absolutely endorse informed consent. I believe that it's extremely important for caregivers to explore all avenues and take ownership of the decisions they make for their child/ren, rather than place responsibility solely in healthcare professionals or be so mistrusting that they block them out altogether. An informed decision comes from hearing and deliberating all sides of the argument. It can be difficult if your instincts go against what you're being told, and it may be difficult for you to feel like you can speak up in this sort of situation.

I highly recommend reading *Hold Your Prem* by Jill Bergman. It contains valuable and progressive information as well as being laid out in a way which makes it easy for caregivers to assimilate the information in bite-size portions if they don't have time to read the chapter in full. It's co-written by Dr. Nils Bergman, who is a kangaroo care expert, so it's a handy book to have to "back up" any decisions you may want to make regarding your baby or babies' care.

Sensory processing disorders

This section deserves a special focus, as:

1) sensory processing disorders are hard to diagnose and;

2) many babies and children will exhibit some symptoms even if they don't have such a disorder

There are lists of different aversions[8] which you can read through and see if any apply to your baby or child. Of course, having aversions doesn't mean that they necessarily have a disorder, but we can certainly look at some of the aversions that may affect carrying and see if we can help with some of them. Again, none of this is designed to replicate or overrule a medical professional's insight, so if you feel like something may work for you, either speak with your healthcare provider first or make the decision to try something from an informed place.

Tactile aversions

Doesn't like to be held or cuddled

They may arch their back, cry, and pull away. The sensory stimulation of touch may be too much for them.

This is a situation where carrying may prove to be difficult, as they may resist being held. Work with your baby/child to figure out if there are specific trigger points for over-stimulation. Things like a retained spinal galant reflex may factor into this aversion, by making support in that area uncomfortable.

If you can't pinpoint an area, try to gauge if they're ok with some physical stimulation or averse to much of it. If they're ok for short periods, work with carrying for this time. You may find that there are certain ways of carrying that they're receptive to, such as supporting just at the legs.

Vestibular issues

May cling excessively to carer

Over-sensitivity to movement may make them cling on hard through fear of the perceived excesses of movement from you. Something you can try is slowing down your movements where possible, to help associate carrying with security rather than a scary ride. A firm hold may also help with their feelings of stability.

May appear to hate being carried

A fear of heights from being disorientated may make carrying virtually impossible. They may protest and resist physically. One thing to try here is using front carries with firm holding, or using a sling facing inwards. Front carrying offers several positives for this sensory issue – limited view of the world around them (and how high they're up), easy visual contact with your face and it being a natural hugging position. There are lots of comforting factors here. This may not work, of course, but it's worth a try!

Limit or completely avoid positions which provide this excessive stimulation, such as facing outwards and also hip carries if they pose a problem.

Floppy body (low muscle tone)

May grab onto you tightly with hands as a way of trying to compensate for lack of other clinging behaviours, and may have issues with self-stabilising to compensate for your movements.

Using passive carries and slowly building up to active carries may help here if the muscle tone is within the realms of improvement. Also, use advice from their healthcare provider to adapt your carrying for your unique dyad.

You know your child better than anyone else – use their cues and your intimate knowledge of their carrying behaviours to work out what's enough or too much for them. Take it slowly too.

Gets tired easily

Do they get tired more easily than other babies/children their age? Do they find active carrying tiring? If they've been engaging in active carrying for a while and don't seem to be gaining stamina, this may be an issue.

You can help them by providing more support when they're tired and building up active carrying more slowly than your body may want to.

Procioceptive dysfunctions

Prefers tight holding

They may prefer a snug sling or carrier to in-arms carrying, needing the firm sensory stimulation.

If you identify this as a symptom, by all means try slightly firmer holding in-arms, whilst respecting their spinal development. You may be able to apply aspects of therapeutic holding – speak to their healthcare provider to find out whether it's appropriate for them.

You may find that you tire more easily, or that their need for tightness is better met with an all-encompassing sling (for their body, not including their head!). Again, work with their needs. Can these be met by having a cuddling session before being carried? If so, you may find you can carry "normally" for some periods of time.

Hates being held facing inwards

An excessive need for visual stimulation may mean they prefer –

and actively seek out – facing forwards when being carried. How do they find hip carries? This can be a great way for them to get more stimulation whilst enabling you to monitor them for signs of over-stimulation. We also tend to be able to facilitate this type of hold for longer than facing forwards.

A mixture of facing forwards, hip carrying and shoulder carrying (when developmentally ready) may work well for a baby with a need for more visual stimulation.

Slow or little response or over-response to your movements

They may find it hard to judge the correct degree of compensation for your movements. This may also be confused with high or low muscle tone.

You may find you need to slow down your speed when using active carrying, to enable them to better process the sensory input from your movements. When you need to move faster you may find passive holds work better.

Self regulation

Requires lots of help with soothing, regulating emotions and help to get to sleep

May show signs of distress a lot of the time, and/or need constant movement to fall asleep.

Most babies require more soothing and movement than we've been led to believe, but if their needs seem off the charts compared to other babies/children their age, there may be a sensory issue present.

Lots of movement when carrying (e.g. swaying, dancing, constant motion etc.) can help with meeting this sensory need. Reassurance, gentle touch and soothing tones of voice are all ways of alleviating stress for them, combined with movement.

Autism spectrum disorders – babies and children

While suspicions of autism spectrum disorders (ASD) may not present until after age 2 in many cases, and diagnosis occurring sometimes years later, it may only be in hindsight that you make connections with differences in carrying.

As it's been suggested from research, it may be possible to diagnose ASD much earlier than is conventionally done.[9] If you notice these signs and/or retained reflexes it may be worth considering mentioning this to your healthcare provider (HCP) so they can advise further.

If you notice abnormalities in the way they are developing, even if it seems to be on track time-wise, please discuss with your HCP. The research mentioned in the previous paragraph notes how all the ASD-present children studied showed abnormalities in their development, such as crawling on one knee and one foot.

Deviations from the agreed norm may not automatically mean there is an issue, but it's always worth getting a second (or third or fourth) opinion to get a fresh perspective. Above all, even if several professionals have told you all is well, if your gut is telling you that something is off, please trust it. Parental instinct is one of the most ignored yet most powerful.

If your baby/child has an ASD, it's worth looking at each symptom and/or developmental deviation individually. By doing this you can recognise how each thing impacts on carrying and work out any adaptations you could make to ensure carrying is impacted less.

When there's no diagnosis

We are the people who care the most about our children's development and are the ones who have the most to lose if we don't recognise the signs that something is off. It may not always be to do with a disorder but even if there isn't something diagnosable, individual issues can affect our child's development. Many children exhibit issues with sensory processing, and even symptoms of other disorders which aren't "enough" for a diagnosis. Being in the grey area of known issues but having no name/diagnosis for them can be lonely and disempowering. Not having an official name for what your child is going through can make supporting them that much harder.

I really encourage you to recognise what you feel is off and to trust your parental insights into how best to support them. Of course this can be incredibly hard with no blueprint on how to proceed, but I feel that tapping into our insights can help us to develop our own plans going forwards.

For instance, one of my children exhibits multiple signs of sensory processing disorder, and some which line up with ASD'S, but they don't tick all the right boxes. I've learnt to address each of the issues without relying on an umbrella diagnosis.

As parents/carers we know these children inside out and we may be able to tailor and fine-tune approaches based on this knowledge plus our sensitivity to what works best for them.

Chapter 15

Troubleshooting

Although everything may seem like it works in perfect harmony on paper, we all know that babies, children and ourselves are individuals. As we've explored, it's not as simple as being born with the ability to do something. Each person has their own unique capacity to grow that skill, and some will find it harder than others. As we just looked at, some people will have different obstacles present. Any capability needs nurturing to reach its full potential.

Carrying tends to be harder from the get go because as a society we're sedentary, and (even if we try to keep our babies and children as active as possible) our little ones follow suit. Keeping on top of the traps of sedentary living can seem overwhelming once you realise its far-reaching effects. Having this awareness, though, can enable you to gradually make changes which will help you with carrying.

Let's look at some common problems and explore possible solutions. As with anything in parenting, take what works for you, discard what doesn't, and trust your own instincts to come up with your own adaptations.

My baby/child seems to slip a lot when I carry them

The first port of call here is to look at the sort of clothing you and they wear. As I mentioned earlier, any clothing which doesn't create friction is going to hinder the carrying process. If both peoples clothing is suited to carrying, then we can look at possible triggers for the slippage.

First, is your baby in the reflexive carrying phase? If so, it's normal for them to drop and raise their leg/s when they're awake and active. Its part of the instinctive repetitive movement patterns they make which leads to integrating the reflexes. If their leg drops but fails to make the corrective movement, keep an eye on it. It's perfectly normal for them to do this occasionally, but if it's constant it may be worth seeing your GP so they can check to see if the reflex is missing.

If it's when they're sleeping, they may need help with their positioning, adjusting them into the foetal tuck or similar. This pelvic tilt keeps the knees higher up, bum lower down, so their body effectively pins their legs against your body. Remember, these reflexes are triggered when they're awake, only occasionally or partially in light sleep, and not at all in deep sleep.

If this is with an older baby or child, paying attention to when you're noticing this can give you a better idea as to what's going on. If it's when they're tired or antsy you may want to consider using a more passive position to give them a break. If its most of the time, have a look at where you're supporting them and how often you change position or where the support is. Depending on their stage of development they may need support in a different area so that it encourages the physiological carrying position. Also, note how long it's been since you adopted active carrying. If it's been only recently, they will need time to adapt to it and build up their clinging capabilities. It can't be rushed.

Baby gets upset or antsy

When your baby gets upset, see if you can pinpoint the trigger for it. This may be difficult if there seems to be nothing obvious going on. Here are some possibilities:

Have they been trying to communicate a need to you?

If so, they may be getting agitated about feeling unheard. Remember the 7 stages of consciousness (see end of book) – communication begins in the most subtle ways and becomes more evident the more frustrated they get.

Do they need to change position?

They can get antsy when they've had enough of sitting in one position. Think about how we sit. We don't usually sit for long in one position if we can help it. We move around to get comfortable, and if we sit for too long we can begin to ache. Although we may be soft and squidgy in some ways, we still have potential pressure points on our bodies which will trigger an attempt at a change of position once the pressure becomes uncomfortable for them. Some babies are more sensitive than others and may experience discomfort more often.

Another possibility is retention of the spinal galant reflex. This reflex causes the hip to swing towards the stimulus (stroking on either side of the spine) and should integrate by nine months. Babies and children with a retained spinal galant reflex tend to get antsy when their lower back is stimulated. If you have any concerns that they are still exhibiting this reflex, please see your healthcare provider.

Do they need to eliminate or have a nappy change?

One of the in-arms cues for needing the toilet (from birth) is wriggling and/or kicking the legs. In the first 5-6 months of life they have an awareness of needing to eliminate. If this communication isn't responded to they gradually lose the awareness of it or the inclination to let you know/be bothered about it. It's hard to say which, as we can't ask them! So the responsiveness to feeling the need to wee or poo gradually wanes until it disappears around 5 or 6 months of age.

They will likely still display their unique behaviours when needing to or doing a poo though, so this should be kept in mind for older babies and nappied children. For "toilet trained" children do bear in mind that the awareness of needing to go can make them antsy too. You may have noticed when they're engrossed in an activity and need to go that they get fidgety or dance around. However you address your babies toileting needs, communicating to them that you hear them telling you they need to go and that it's ok to pee or poo is always a positive thing. It builds up communication, trust, and a different layer to your relationship.

Are they tired?

Sometimes tired babies need a change of movement (e.g. rocking or bouncing) to settle down in-arms. Sometimes they need to have an ear to your chest to calm them with the sound of your heartbeat. Other times they may need either less or more contact, meaning possibly not being touched/put down/going in a bed or pram, or needing firmer pressure hugged or being enveloped in a sling. Or maybe they need milk to help them settle to sleep? You will know your baby/child's individual needs, so have a think about their personal preferences.

Are they over-stimulated?

Babies and children (babies especially) tend to be sensitive to stimulation from the world around them. Sensory overload can happen, which may make them upset or antsy. The need for regulation of their negative response to the stimulus makes them seek out comfort from their caregiver. If we've not recognised that they're overwhelmed it can make the experience worse for them (and us!). Notice their behaviour – what is it telling you? If you're unsure, have a look at the environment you're in. Is it busy? Noisy? Bright? Disorientating?

How are you holding them? If they're facing out, try holding them facing in. If they're on your hip, try on your front, preferably offering them the chance to rest their head on your chest so they can hear your heartbeat. If they're on your back, bring them to your front so they can see you. Even being in physical contact isn't always enough – seeing your face can be very calming and anchoring for them.

If you think they're over-stimulated and trying out different positions and trying to calm them doesn't work, you may want to consider leaving the source of over-stimulation.

How can I feed comfortably in-arms?

Feeding is most definitely possible when carrying in-arms. For younger babies, you'll find the primitive reflexes aid this, and as they grow they should adapt to feeding on the go. That being said, it's worth mentioning that in the early days and weeks babies are designed to feed better with the caregiver in a position of rest. Yes, it's possible to adapt to busy lifestyles, but you will get the best response by following their natural behaviours.

That said, I'm not your mum so I'm not going to tell you what you "should" do! You're a grown adult who knows what you want or need, and are more than capable of adapting to your situation. So here's some information which I hope will help you along.

In the early weeks the reflexes which aid feeding carrying positions are similar to upright carrying - the difference is how they present in feeding behaviour. You may have heard about, or seen videos of, the breast crawl. This is where a newborn baby is placed on the stomach of the gestational parent or a lactating parent's stomach and proceeds to "crawl" to the breast.[1] The "crawling" action is a great one to observe, not only to see how a newborn seeks out milk from smell and reflexive moving, but for noticing how the reflexes used in carrying are engaged in this too.

The newborn is able to "crawl" because the smell of the milk triggers them to lift their head towards the smell (head bobs up and down), and the head lifting places more pressure further down their body, triggering a forward propulsion from their upper body (supported by their forearms) and from the jerking up of the knee/s from stimulation of the foot on the caregiver's body.

This seems almost a miracle, seeing as babies tend not to move from point A to point B until they've developed at least the skill to roll. But this shows some of the potential of reflexes in action, and as you will see (and have seen with regular carrying), the reflexes tend to work in synchronicity when performing an action. It's just the scientific approach which singles the reflexes out and gives them individual classifications.

Moving on from the biological nursing position (often called "biological nurturing") let's look at other reflexes linked to feeding and some different positions used to feed.

Babkin reflex This reflex is elicited by pressing palms on both palms, and results in the baby opening their mouth. This can be useful if the baby is getting frustrated at the breast or bottle and is having trouble latching on.

Palmar reflex When sucking, babies grip harder when the palmar reflex is activated. This could be seen as a natural progression from the Babkin reflex – keeping hold of the hands once latched. In carrying this serves a great purpose – instead of being completely distracted by milk and putting all their energy into sucking, they are protected by being able to hold on tighter.

Spread-squat reflex With young babies reflexively bringing their knees up when on their back or being picked up, it enables positions such as the rugby hold (or football hold if you're an American reader) to work well. As the baby makes contact with the caregiver's side, the knees raise and "hook" round their body. So much easier to hold than having dangling legs, right?

Cradle hold A very popular breast- and bottle-feeding position is the cradle hold. In this position the baby has one leg higher than the other.

Cross cradle hold[2] This differs from the cradle hold in that you use the opposite arm to support your baby.

You can usually adapt feeding positions to work for you both on the go, but you may find some don't work, either due to being unable to support them well enough or them not liking it.

In carrying, work with the positions which keep your baby most securely attached to your body. Remember to keep complete bodily contact with each other – this helps them to feel stable and enables them to coordinate their movements.[3] Also remember to keep their body aligned well.

With young babies you can work with the reflexes to encourage better clinging behaviour, and with older babies you can help them to learn to hold themselves in ways which makes it easier for you to support them, or work with the clinging reflexes for upright carrying. Remember to take care with how you're holding your body too, as it's easy to slip into bad habits.

Bottle feeding on the go may require a bit of adaptation as you're required to hold the bottle with one of your hands, but is still very much possible. You will just need to adapt your preferred ways of holding to enable you to provide support with one arm and holding the bottle with the other.

It's important with all in-arms feeding to recognise that extra attention is needed to keep an eye on baby's airways. Make sure there is always adequate support to keep their chin off their chest. In the early weeks, and whenever they're sleepy or asleep at any age, they're at a higher risk of positional asphyxiation.

As you can see, feeding on the go is both possible and sometimes essential. As babies are clinging young, nature has it figured out with how we can adapt to feeding on the go!

I keep getting shoulder pain on the side I'm supporting my baby/child with – what's going on?

The next time you're carrying, check how you're supporting them. Check straight away, then a bit later, once you've been carrying a while. As you know, we tend to slip into bad habits when we're not concentrating on how we're holding our body. You may find that you're starting out bearing the weight in the right place but over time you slip into bearing on your ligaments. Or, you may be bearing in the right place but the position of your shoulder may be causing stress to the trapezius. If this is the case, be extra mindful of this area when you're carrying. Eventually you shouldn't need to spend so much time focusing on it, once the new, better habit is formed!

If you can't see anything wrong in how you're supporting them, please seek medical advice, as you may have an underlying issue.

My baby seems rigid – I find in-arms carrying difficult because s/he doesn't relax into me

First of all, is this all the time or some of the time? If it's just some of the time, you could try making notes on when this is. Is it just after a feed? Is it when they're upset? Does it happen when there's a lot going on around them? Is it accompanied by back-arching?

If the rigidity is most of the time and you can't pinpoint a trigger or triggers, there are a few options for you to consider. There may be a problem that can be fixed such as muscular tension in the body. The birth process can affect babies, especially if there was any trauma involved. Even in seemingly normal births things like positioning and the duration of the birth can affect the baby. Caesarean sections may sometimes present issues too, such as how the baby was handled coming out and missing the process of primitive reflex triggers as they enter and navigate the birth canal.

Consulting with your doctor, an osteopath or a chiropractor may give you some answers. Osteopaths and chiropractors who are trained to treat babies will be better able to diagnose and treat muscle tensions and/or postural issues as they are trained in this body work. You may find your GP doesn't offer much insight into muscular issues as their training is more general but they are definitely a good option to rule out other potential problems such as hypertonia, GERD or intolerances.

If you've explored all these possibilities and still have no answer, maybe you would like to consider exploring baby massage and/or seeing if they're still tense in a sling (try firmer and less firm holds to see if they respond to tactile stimulation).

My baby seems floppy and doesn't seem to participate in carrying

Again, is this some of the time or most/all of the time? See if you can identify a pattern for when this happens, if it's not all of the time. If it's some of the time, it's likely to be linked to sleepiness.

If s/he's floppy most or all of the time, it's worth taking them to your GP for assessment. Hypotonia (low muscle tone) is something which has varying degrees and may also be a symptom of another problem. Depending on the severity, hypotonia may be able to be improved.

If your baby does have low muscle tone it's best to discuss with your healthcare provider about the appropriate course of action. If it's severe enough to not improve you will find that you can still work out ways of carrying to suit you both. Using the precautions for newborn and sleeping babies, along with more passive positions and considering using a sling too will keep you close and give you options which you can adapt to suit your family.

For low muscle tone and in-arms carrying, you can take precautions such as:

- Providing extra support around the nape of their neck and upper back when lifting and carrying them

- Being aware of how balanced they are – making sure their body and head aren't twisted

- Ensuring that there isn't an uneven distribution of their weight – that it is borne equally on both sides

- Using two arms to support them if needed – one for the lower body and one for the upper

I have a pre-existing back/neck/shoulder problem – how can I carry comfortably?

First of all, refer to the advice given to you by the person overseeing your care. What have they said about lifting and weight-bearing? Are you able to adapt this advice to work out how best to carry? If you've not been advised about this, please speak to them as they will have knowledge of your condition and how carrying loads may affect it. If you've not seen someone about the problem, please do!

If you need to make do in the meantime, I would suggest avoiding load-bearing in that area to be on the safe side. Remember that the hips and shoulders are connected, left to right and right to left.

If you babywear, you may already have knowledge of what works best for your body in terms of where is comfortable on your body and how high or low you need to carry. You may be able to use this knowledge to help work out what's best for you in-arms, but do remember that babywearing isn't in-arms carrying with something tied on. They work in different ways and weight bears in different places depending on how you're carrying. What work in slings/carriers may be very uncomfortable and vice-versa.

I'm finding carrying uncomfortable. I've used all the principles and tips and I still hurt

Are you uncomfortable all the time or just at certain times? If it's occasionally, could you note when this is and what you've been doing in the 48hrs prior to the uncomfortable carrying? How about afterwards? Sometimes we can throw our bodies out by doing things we're not used to, as we're using muscles that don't usually get that sort of use. Also, with regular activities, we may overdo it sometimes.

Even sleeping funny can mess with your body! The way I subconsciously position myself means I occasionally mess my neck and/or upper back up. This can obviously be confused with doing something else, such as carrying the day before, if you're not aware of this possibility. You're one of the best people to know whether it's carrying related or not, as you'll know how you've been carrying, where exactly within your body you're hurting, if you're only hurting when you're carrying etc.

If it's regularly and you've tried everything, please see a doctor. You may have an underlying issue that you're not aware of. Carrying should not be uncomfortable.

I enjoy carrying in-arms but I find it really difficult when my baby falls asleep in them

There are a few solutions to this, depending on how your baby responds when sleeping, and your needs and circumstances. First up is putting them down, which may seem obvious! It will obviously depend on where you are, if they stay asleep when you put them down and your own wants and needs. If you find they wake as soon as you put them down, you might want to try the following:

- Keep close bodily contact as you lower them down, keeping their tummy to your body until laying on the surface, then slowly moving your body away whilst placing your hand on their chest – once just your hand is on there, gradually lessen contact until you're not touching anymore

- Placing a blanket around their back before putting them down – you might want to incorporate the above, while wrapping the blanket around them snugly

If it's not possible to put them down because they wake, you could either sit (slightly reclined) or lay with them on your chest instead. This may not be practical all the time, I know, but is still an option, especially if you need some rest yourself or you have something you can do seated.

Another option is to either tie a sling around you both once s/he's asleep, or pop them in one when they exhibit their sleepy cues. It can be easier for them to go to sleep in slings sometimes, and cuts out the need to transfer them to a bed or similar.

If you're out and about and have nothing on you to aid you (sling, pushchair, someone else's arms etc.) you will need to think about how you're carrying them. Are you finding it hard because they're suddenly a dead weight, or are you using your body in unnatural positions to brace their weight? Do you need to provide support in different areas, or might it be more comfortable if you changed position?

For example, do you need to use your hand to support their neck, or do you feel like you need to use both arms to support their weight? You could hold them up to your shoulder in an off-centre hold (remembering not to arch your back!) so that their head can rest on your shoulder. Or maybe you could hold them on your front and use one arm to support their legs and bum, and the other to support their upper back.

Are you in a position to stop somewhere? Do you have anything on you which you could improvise with and turn into a carrying aid? For example, baggy hoodies and cardigans can easily be turned into an aid by doing them up around the baby/child and tucking some of the material knee to knee. These are *never* hands-free options though – they will just take some of the load as you carry, and can sometimes aid somewhat with neck support.

If none of these are options in the moment, you may need to plan ahead so that you have something to aid you in future, but for now you can refer to the tips for low muscle tone babies for when they're asleep.

A word of caution

Some babies may present symptoms which may seem to indicate a certain diagnosis. This may not always be the case, and it's wise to see your healthcare provider if you have any concerns about your baby/child's health.

Even if there's no diagnosis, if your little one exhibits certain behaviours you may find that using tips provided helps your carrying journey. You also know your own child better than anyone else, so don't be scared to use the principles for safe and comfortable carrying and come up with your own adaptations!

Conclusion

Well, there you have it! I think its clear how important in-arms carrying is, and how it links to different stages of development. I hope you agree with me, and will encourage the expansion of this new (but ancient) area. Much of what I could have added to this book was either very controversial (theories into the impact of our lifestyles including lack of carrying) or not close enough to what I wanted to focus on – things like comparing human behaviours with that of apes and other primates, or comparing carrying in cultures who have never succumbed to modern-day "convenience" (a.k.a. body-ruining devices).

There is so much more that could be speculated on, enough to fill at least a couple more books, but I wanted to focus on culture-specific and species-specific information where possible. I didn't want to dilute the carrying message by theorising about different species of animals, or daydream about what carrying may look like if we hadn't abandoned physiological practices. I wanted to draw a focus to the need to highlight where our society has gone wrong in its desperation to "advance", to show how we and our children are being harmed by this need, and to show that there is still hope of reversing what damage has already been done.

As I've banged on about, I believe in-arms carrying is a developmental process in and of itself, that requires further study. If nothing else, learning more about in-arms carrying can make it more comfortable for the person doing the carrying, and potentially protect their body. If I had two wishes (because one wouldn't include the second) they would be that as many people as possible would learn more about the benefits of in-arms carrying, and that there would be a new awareness in the scientific world about the importance of carrying, and how it's a valid developmental phase. I truly hope that this book will find its way into the right hands to trigger some wonderful carrying-specific research. If one caregiver decides to carry in-arms more, this work has been worth it. If one scientist decides to conduct research into one of the points of interest of in-arms carrying, many more people will benefit.

Because of the lack of in-depth information of carrying throughout history, we don't have a clear picture of the ramifications of not encouraging natural clinging behaviour. In fact, the lack of active carrying in the majority of people here means that the impact of it is our current "normal". It would be interesting to see some studies conducted to find out what the potential "benefits" are of encouraging clinging behaviour. I use the word benefits in quotation marks because they really wouldn't be benefits, but the norm for human clinging young.

While there are cultures around the world that haven't lost this knowledge, I feel we need to be careful about making comparisons. I've purposely avoided deepening a general history of in-arms carrying in the first chapter due to how I feel about this. I've many reasons, including:

We have no right

This is the biggest one. We have no right to intrude on other cultures for our own benefit. Maybe some people would be happy to participate in studies, but that's up to the individual people. This is a big reason why I've stuck to my own culture within this book, and not drawn comparisons outside of it.
There certainly are pictures on the internet which show people in traditional cultures carrying their babies in-arms, but there's no indication as to whether these have been taken with consent, and many have watermarks, suggesting they've been taken for profit. I'm not going to perpetuate using marginalised people for observation without their consent and compensation.

It's not my lane

All the cultures I've come across that haven't succumbed to modern "conveniences" are outside of my heritage. I know I don't have the credentials that some place more value on (whether related to the topic at hand or not), but I do have lived experience of my own culture and day to day observations of how my culture in general lives and carries their children.

This makes me happy to talk about the subject from this point of view. It would be a disservice to other cultures to attempt to discuss carrying from an outside perspective. The experts are those living in these cultures, and if anyone decides to share their knowledge and wisdom, I look forward to buying their book/course/other offering!

We're so long past what is biologically normal for our culture

Even if we obtain consent, how can we compare our carrying habits to a culture which has preserved carrying, when we have no real point of reference as to what is normal for ourselves? Sure, we could make generalisations but it's well known that people all around the world live differently to one another. We know that natives from different countries can have markedly different bone structures and body types, as well as having actively different daily lives, so what is normal for one may not be for another.

We may be able to draw some useful information, but humans live differently in different areas

This is especially important when we think about how we in the UK tend to ruin our bodies over the years, but those in some other cultures preserve normal bodily motion/movement. A person who has perfect posture and lives with minimal furniture (or furniture-free) and has an active lifestyle occasionally holding out of alignment is going to impact their body differently to someone with postural and/or alignment issues.
We can't think about applying the norm elsewhere without getting our own cultural norm back to what is *biologically* normal for humans. If we succeeded in getting back to that point, would we even need to look outside of our own culture?

After all that's said and done, I believe it's important for us to acknowledge that we live in a time where "advancement" is classified in terms of how little we have to do and how advanced technology is. To do this, and encourage the passing down of knowledge and skills through our families, will enable our "normal" to get back to the *real* normal.

Knowing that babies and children are incredibly resilient and are built to withstand our questionable choices, that even through periods of time where parents have unknowingly harmed their babies/children in various ways, we seem to have survived impeccably. This is shown by the way most babies are born healthy and develop well, and that it's only as they grow older that we tend to see the impact on their bodies.

Realizing that over many hundreds of years our ancestors have paved the path to where we are now, by placing more value on the patriarchy and the things that concerned them, war and the "advancement" of society than the knowledge and wisdom of mothers, grandmothers and other knowledgeable people. Understanding that change is possible in our hands and we hold the power to improve the lives of our children and grandchildren.

Going forwards I believe we need to learn more, circulate that knowledge, get this (and so many more parenting practices) back to where it belongs – being passed on family to family. Of course there's a period of time needed to pass on this knowledge and search for more information outside of the family setup, but (like babywearing and doula'ing) it's something where my ultimate aim is to do myself out of a job.

I hope you've found this book both enjoyable and useful, and that it's planted a seed in you, ready to germinate, passing on what you've learned and/ or adding your knowledge to the collective pool to help our understanding grow. I hope you may be one of the people who brings more knowledge to the table and helps further our understanding in this area. Remember, even if you feel like there are people out there who know a lot more than you, you will *always* bring something valuable to the table. Have faith, and share your message!

If you've found this book interesting and would like to join in discussion about in-arms carrying, please join us at **In-arms Carrying Discussion Group – UK**. Here you will also find links to other groups around the world!

If you'd like to explore the information in this book further, in an interactive setting, I offer a short course and a full course (online self-study), which you can find at:

www.inarmscarrying.com

The short course is designed as CPD study, and is useful for professionals to deepen their understanding of carrying as a developmental process and the different stages of development. It includes educational videos relating to reflexes and carrying, and you get lifetime access to the content.

The full course is designed for professionals who want to take their learning further and actively work with parents and carers to help them carry comfortably and in ways that benefit both them and the baby/child. This could be through carrying-specific classes and/or consultations, or to compliment a service they already provide (Babywearing Consultant, antenatal teachers, doulas etc.).

Included is a full online toolkit of videos, presentations and graphics for you to use in your work, as well as a private Facebook group for discussion and support. You have lifetime access to the content, which means you benefit from any updated or additional content in the future!

When all's said and done, it's great to have more information, new angles to approach our parenting from, but the reality is that society and life in general makes it far from easy for us. If you're able to implement lots of what I've discussed, that's fantastic and I'm excited for you and your child/ren. If your life doesn't enable you to do as much as you want to do for your child/ren (and/or yourself), please don't beat yourself up about it. Life is about gaining the knowledge to make informed choices for our personal circumstances. I can tell you right now that my knowledge and experience of in-arms carrying and this book could easily have been miles better if I'd had the time to devote the past 4 years to full-time studying, recording and writing about all my observations of carrying.

Some people are able to work out ways to change their living situations to better their family's health, but others are trapped in situations with no light at the end of the tunnel. Know better, do better doesn't always work. Some people are barely surviving day to day, and have to prioritise. There's no place for judgement. I'm a classic example of knowing what I should do and not doing it.

With regards to this book, I hope it's useful and provides some starting points and different ideas to explore further. I'm proud of my work and where I've gone with carrying yet I know that there are many more people out there who are more focused, have more time on their hands and are highly trained in relevant areas that I'm not. I'm waiting in anticipation for the wonderful expansions they can provide on in-arms carrying with their dedication and knowledge, qualitative and quantitative research, and I look forward to learning more.

I just want to leave you with this: If we want to improve our children's, grandchildren's and nation's health then we have a responsibility to do what we can and use our knowledge, experiences and privileges to shape the future. Please do your bit to normalise in-arms carrying and help the next generation suffer less physically – we can make a massive impact if we all do our fair share.

P.S. If you find any errors or discrepancies in this book, or want to share any thoughts you have, please feel free to drop me a line at: hello@melcyrille.com

Citations

Chapter 1

[1] *Babydoo infographic -*
http://www.babydoousa.com/babywearing-in-the-first-year/

[2] *In-arms carrying and babywearing -*
http://www.tribalbabies.co.uk/in-arms-carrying-and-babywearing/

[3] *Katy Bowman's website –* www.nutritiousmovement.com

[4] *Baby holding without shoulder straining -*
https://www.youtube.com/watch?v=904_CkMqkmo

[5] *Pain free baby holding -*
https://www.youtube.com/watch?v=R3H2R5Nn38g

[6] *Baby Carrying Can Affect Cervical Spine: A Study of Two Designs* BB Zietsman, AI Heusch, PW McCarthy (2015)

[7] *The Effects of Load Carriage on Spinal Curvature and Posture* Heidi A. Orloff, Catherine M. Rapp (2004)

[8] *The effects of body posture by using Baby Carrier in different ways* Kim, Kyoung; Yun, Ki Hyun (2013)

Chapter 2

[1] Sim, Alison (1998). *The Tudor Housewife.* McGill-Queen's Press. p. 26. ISBN 978-0-7509-3774-0.

[2] *Much Ado About Babies* (2013)

[3] *Does Swaddling Influence Developmental Dysplasia of the Hip?* Susan T. Mahan & James R. Kasser

[4] *Screening for developmental dysplasia of the hip: results of a 7-year follow-up study* Sahin F, Aktu¨ rk A, Beyazova U, et al. (2004)

[5] *Clinical examination versus ultrasonography in detecting developmental dysplasia of the hip* Dogruel H, Atalar H, Yavuz OY, Sayli U. (2007)

[6] *The pattern of developmental dysplasia of the hip* Kremli MK, Alshahid AH, Khoshhal KI, Zamzam MM (2003)

[7] *The Emotional Life of Nations* by Lloyd deMause

[8] *A Handbook of obstetric nursing for nurses, students and mothers* by Anna Martha Fullerton, Philidelphia - https://books.google.co.uk/books?ei=m52JUN6uAcaB0QG6 hoHYBw&redir_esc=y&id=P6IH1ff88nEC&focus=searchwithi nvolume&q=tyrant

[9] *Distribution and determinants of sedentary lifestyles in the European Union* J Varo, M Martínez-González, J Irala-Estévez, J Kearney, M Gibney, J Martínez. Int J Epidemiol (2003)

[10] *Beloved Burden – Baby-wearing around the world* by I.C. Van Hoult

[11] Woven wrap - https://southlondonslings.co.uk/2012/07/05/woven-wrap-as-a-traditional-english-baby-sling/

[12] *Das Tragen des Sauglings im Huftsitz – eine spezielle Anpassung des menschlichen Traglings (Carrying the infant sitting on the mother's hip - A special adaptation of the clinging*

young) Kirkilionis, Evelin

[13] *Cache or Carry?* http://bindungtraegt.de/cache-or-carry-comparative-biology-and-infant-carrying/

[14] Bernard Hassenstein (clinging young research 1970, 2007)

Chapter 3

[1] *The Biobehavioral Effects of Gentle Human Touch on Preterm Infants* Mary Anne Modrcin-Talbott, Lynda Law Harrison, Maureen W. Groer, Mary Sue Younger (2003)

[2] *The Neurosequential Model of Therapeutics* Bruce D. Perry and Erin P. Hambrick (2006)

[3] *The Use of Human Touch to Improve the Well-Being of Older Adults - A Holistic Nursing Intervention* Elizabeth Bush (2001)

[4] *Infant Crying and Maternal Responsiveness* Ainsworth, Bell (1972)

[5] 7 Stages of Consciousness, Back of book

[6] *Infants' Somatotopic Neural Responses to Seeing Human Actions: I've Got You under My Skin* Joni N. Saby, Andrew N. Meltzoff, Peter J. Marshall (2013)

[7] *Hierarchy of Needs* Abraham Maslow (1943, 1954)

[8] *How Important Is Physical Contact with Your Infant?* Katherine Harman (2010)

[9] *Calming Effects of Deep Touch Pressure in Patients with Autistic Disorder, College Students, and Animals* Temple Grandin (2009)

[10] *Chest skin temperature of mothers of term and preterm infants is higher than that of men and women* K Bauer, K Pasel, H Versmold Paediatric Research (1996)

[11] *Hold Your Prem* Jill Bergman (page 51)

[12] *Hold Your Prem* Jill Bergman (page 52)

[13] *Breast-infant temperature synchrony with twins during shared kangaroo care* Ludington-Hoe et al (2006)

[14] *Infant Calming Responses during Maternal Carrying in Humans and Mice* G Esposito et al (2013)

[15] *Frequency of Infant Stroking Reported by Mothers Moderates the Effect of Prenatal Depression on Infant Behavioural and Physiological Outcomes* Sharp H, Pickles A, Meaney M, Marshall K, Tibu F, and Hill J. (2012)

Maternal antenatal anxiety, postnatal stroking and emotional problems in children: outcomes predicted from pre- and postnatal programming hypotheses Sharp H, Hill J, Hellier J, NS Pickles A. (2014)

[16] *Ätiologie, Prophylaxe und Frühbehandlung der Luxationshüfte (Etiology, prevention and early treatment of dislocation of hip dysplasia)* Büschelberger (1964)

[17] Early Human Development (2013)

[18] *Metabolic cost of generating muscular force in human walking: insights from load-carrying and speed experiments* Timothy M. Griffin, Thomas J. Roberts, and Rodger Kram

[19] *Infant Carrying: The Role of Increased Locomotory Costs in Early Tool Development* CM Wall-Scheffler, K Geiger, KL Steudel-Numbers (2007)

Chapter 4

[1] *Untersuchungen über Eigenart des Hüftgelenks im Säuglingsalter und ihre Bedeutung für die Pathogenese, Prophylaxe und Therapie der Luxationshüfte* Büschelberger (1961)

[2] *Baby Wants to be Carried* Evelin Kirkilionis

[3] *Etiology, pathogenesis and possible prevention of congenital dislocation of the hip* R. B. Salter (1968)

[4] NHS - http://www.nhs.uk/conditions/developmental-dysplasia-of-the-hip/Pages/Introduction.aspx

[5] *Hüftdysplasie: Sinnvolle Hilfe für Babyhüften* Fettweis (2004)

[6] See reference 2

[7] See Chapter 3, reference 1

[8] See chapter 2, reference 5

Chapter 5

[1] *Eshkol-Wachman movement notation in diagnosis: the early detection of Asperger's syndrome* Teitelbaum, O.; Benton, T.; Shah, P. K.; Prince, A.; Kelly, J. L.; Teitelbaum, P. (2004)

[2] *Primary reflex persistence in children with reading difficulties (dyslexia): A cross-sectional study* Julie-Ann Jordan-Black, Martin McPhillips

[3] *Primitive Reflexes and Attention-Deficit/Hyperactivity Disorder: Developmental Origins of Classroom Dysfunction* M Taylor, S Houghton, E Chapman (2004)

[4] *Rhythmic Movement Training* Harold Blomberg
Movements that Heal Harold Blomberg

[5] WEIRD - https://en.wikipedia.org/wiki/Psychology#Contemporary_issues_in_methodology_and_practice

[6] *Locomotor Primitives in Newborn Babies and Their Development* Nadia Dominici et al. (2011)

Chapter 8

[1] *Use of backpacks in children and adolescents: a potential contributor of back pain* MR Rateau (2004)

The effect of backpacks on the lumbar spine in children: a standing magnetic resonance imaging study TB Neuschwander, J Cutrone, BR Macias, S Cutrone (2010)

Chapter 9

[1] *The effect of posture on the lumbar spine* Adams MA, Hutton WC (1985)

[2] *Postural effects of symmetrical and asymmetrical loads on the spines of schoolchildren* Stefano Negrini, Alberto Negrini (2007)

Posture and the compressive strength of the lumbar spine M.A.Adams PhD, D.S.McNally PhD, H.Chinn BSc, P.Dolan PhD (1993)

[3] See chapter 3, reference 6

[4] *Carrying and Spine Loading* J.D. Rose, E. Mendel, W.S. Marras (2013)

[5] Up with gravity - http://www.upwithgravity.net/up-with-gravitysm-lesson-1-locating-your-center-of-gravity/

[6] See chapter 3, reference 4

[7] *Forward head posture correction* - http://posturedirect.com/forward-head-posture-correction/

[8] *RUA Rib Thruster?* - https://nutritiousmovement.com/rua-rib-thruster/

Chapter 10

[1] *Baby Carriers, Seats and other Equipment (IHDI Educational Statement)* - http://hipdysplasia.org/developmental-dysplasia-of-the-hip/prevention/baby-carriers-seats-and-other-equipment/

[2] *Your Baby's Posture in Baby Gear: Safe and Healthy Infant Positioning* - http://www.candokiddo.com/news/babyposture

[3] *Happy Little Soles* – www.happylittlesoles.co.uk

[4] See chapter 8, reference 1

[5] *Too Much Sitting: The Population-Health Science of Sedentary Behavior* Neville Owen, Geneviève N Healy, Charles E. Matthews, David W. Dunstan (2010)

[6] *Sitting and Sedentary Behaviour are Bad For Your Health* - http://www.nhs.uk/Livewell/fitness/Pages/sitting-and-sedentary-behaviour-are-bad-for-your-health.aspx

[7] *On muscle, tendon and high heels*
R. Csapo, C. N. Maganaris, O. R. Seynnes, M. V. Narici (2010)

[8] *Effect of positive heel inclination on posture*
Franklin ME, Chenier TC, Brauninger L, Cook H, Harris S.

[9] *Emerging issues - Children, mobility and environmental health* - http://www.who.int/ceh/risks/cehmobility/en/

[10] *Bouncing Back? An ethnographic study exploring the context of care and recovery after birth through the experiences and voices of mothers* Julie Wray (2011)

Chapter 11

[1] See Chapter 2, reference 19

[2] *Postural adjustments while standing with two types of loaded backpack* D. Bloom & A. P. Woodhull-Mcneal (1986)

Chapter 12

[1] *Sling Pages* - www.slingpages.co.uk

Chapter 13

[1] *Effects of forward head posture on forced vital capacity and respiratory muscles activity* Jintae Han, Soojin Park, Youngju Kim, Yeonsung Choi, Hyeonnam Lyu

[2] *Mechanics and Energetics of Walking at Different Stride Rates* Brian R. Umberger, Philip E. Martin

[3] *Repetitive strain symptoms -* http://www.nhs.uk/Conditions/Repetitive-strain-injury/Pages/Introduction.aspx

Chapter 14

[1] *Why pregnant women don't tip over -* http://news.nationalgeographic.com/news/2007/12/071212-pregnancy-tips_2.html

[2] *The Influence of Pregnancy on the Location of the Center of Gravity in Standing Position* Agnieszka Opala-Berdzik, Bogden Bacik, Joanna Cieślińska-Świder, Michał Plewa, Monika Gajewska (2010)

[3] *Birth Trauma Association -* http://www.birthtraumaassociation.org.uk/

PANDAS - http://www.pandasfoundation.org.uk/

Mind - https://www.mind.org.uk/information-support/types-of-mental-health-problems/postnatal-depression-and-perinatal-mental-health/ptsd-and-birth-trauma/#.WbPDnoWcHIU

[4] *Vija* - https://www.vija-design.co.uk/

[5] *Premature Babies' Brains Respond Differently to Gentle Touching* Linda Geddes (2017)

[6] *Pain in Neonates is Different* C. Celeste Johnson, Ananda M. Fernandes, Marsha Campbell-Yeo (2010)

[7] *The evolution of primitive reflexes in extremely premature infants* Allen MC, Capute AJ. (1986)

[8] *Sensory processing disorder checklist* - http://www.sensory-processing-disorder.com/sensory-processing-disorder-checklist.html

[9] *Earliest Marker for Autism Found in Young Infants* National Institute of Mental Health (NIMH) Press Release (2013)

Movement analysis in infancy may be useful for early diagnosis of autism Phillip Teitelbaum, Osnat Teitelbaum, Jennifer Nye, Joshua Fryman, Ralph G. Maurer (1998)

Chapter 15

[1] *Breast crawl* - https://www.youtube.com/watch?v=2SX_EWVFqxE

[2] *Cross cradle hold* - https://www.youtube.com/watch?v=MA4kPi-8u_M

[3] *Positioning and attachment* - https://www.laleche.org.uk/positioning-attachment/

7 stages of consciousness/stages of awareness

The following is reproduced from the blog post "How Understanding 7 States of Consciousness Can Transform Your Babywearing Experience" by Mel Cyrille.

1) *Deep (quiet) sleep* – you know this one, where your beautiful one is slumbering peacefully, totally gone.

2) *Light (active) sleep* – this is the time when you're either glad they're finally finished napping, or desperately praying the neighbours/toddler/children/dog/cat/tiniest noise doesn't wake them! They startle in their sleep at noises and twitch or make some movements.

3) *Drowsiness* – that point in time where you feel either huge relief or smile at them with love, watching the huge yawns, eye-rubbing, droopy eyelids and the few seconds here and there of beginning to nod off.

4) *Quiet alert* – your little one is totally chilled out, quiet, peaceful and content. They don't move much, if at all, and seem to be drinking everything in as they gaze at the world.

5) *Active alert* – this is where they're stretching their arms and legs, making those heart-melting gurgles and cooing sounds, look around lots and are generally quite active. In this state they will signal in different ways what – if any – their needs are.

6) *Fussing* – fussing is usually included in the active alert state, but I feel it needs to be separate as they're not in that state because they're fussing. This state comes when their earlier

attempts to tell you they needed haven't been seen, so they then start getting more persistent and vocal about it!

7) *Crying* – when your baby has had enough of communicating in other ways, they reach the last resort…..bawling. They move frantically, screw their face up in upset, and make sure everyone knows there's something wrong!

Acknowledgements

Oh my, this could get very long! There are so many people to thank for this book being birthed, and I don't want to leave anyone out. I will shamelessly shout from the rooftops about the wonderful people who've inspired me – what better way to tell the world than through a book acknowledgement?!

First and foremost, without my husband and children this book could not exist. My children – Niamh, Logan, Xander and Isaac - are my greatest educators in life, and without them I have no idea where I would be right now. They've opened my heart, introduced me to ideas I would never have thought I would consider, and challenged me (every…single…day). They've opened my eyes to new possibilities and ideas, and steered my life-course towards some of the most incredible people I've ever had the privilege to meet – especially the Ipswich Sling Library team who've enabled me to continue with the service over the past 5.5 years.

Thank you Niamh for being my photographer and videographer – your talents are greatly appreciated! It's been lovely sharing this journey with you and I'm proud of what we've achieved together. Thank you to Logan, Xander and Isaac for being my test subjects as well as offering insights independently. My children, you are all kinds of awesome, and don't you ever forget that.

My husband, Tom, has made this book possible not only by making some amazing babies with me, but by supporting me through the ups and downs of parenthood and the "pregnancy" and "birth" of this book. Thank you for your belief in me, encouragement and beer/wine. I love you very much and appreciate everything you've done to make this book possible!

My grandmother, Dorothy, has also been a huge factor in this happening. She's one of my greatest supporters and someone I know is always there for me, no matter what. Nanny, your unwavering support and love has propelled me through the some of the worst of times during the months of writing (and re-writing!) and given me belief in myself. Your words of wisdom keep me grounded, and your faith in me keeps me determined to do you proud. Thank you also for your unfailing help when it comes to technological disasters! I love you very much.

Shaughn and Cerys - without you both I wouldn't have been introduced to slings, and – ultimately – taken this path down the in-arms road. Thank you for all of your wonderful examples of normal parenting practices and your positive influences on my family's choices.

Ali, my wonderful friend, your slingmeet welcomed me into a newfound village of friendship, love and support when Logan was a baby, and introduced me to a wider world of slings, which would lead me to in-arms carrying. Thank you for always being supportive and being the best friend a person could ask for – you're amazing, inspiring and I love you!

Thank you, Kerry, for having tremendous amounts of belief in me as I prepared to launch my own carrying consultancy course through Carried. Your unwavering belief and faith in my abilities got me through that and through writing this book. I love how your daughter is so inclined to clinging behaviour too – her antics have provided smiles and laughs during the times I seriously wanted to throw the towel in with this.

Thank you Ulrika for taking the huge gamble to employ me as a speaker at the first Swedish Babywearing Conference – your belief in my ideas without having any material from me definitely helped get me through some of the hardest times in getting this book out. Your thoughts and comments when I shared the first half of this book with you lifted me more than you will ever know, and your passion for the in-arms message is inspiring.

Anthea and Pixie, thank you so much for your honest thoughts, input and proofreading skills that have helped me to shape this book into something better than it was. Thank you also for your unwavering support and belief in me, especially during the wobbly times.

Thank you Bekki and Izzy, Gina and James, and Faye and Violet for modelling for pictures and videos – you've enabled me to record crucial information for this book and my courses. It was such a pleasure working with you and your beautiful babies!

I also want to thank Olga, from Trageschule, for igniting a passion in me for babywearing when I took my first Babywearing Consultancy course and Lorette from Slingababy for encouraging me to not stick to the "rules". You both helped me in this direction, to this subject that's filled me with so much joy and wonderment.

Thank you all for nudging me in your unique ways towards studying something I find so interesting – it's enriched my life more than you will probably ever know!

Printed in Great Britain
by Amazon